UNIVERSITY OF GLASGOW
PRESS

GUSTAV HOLST

LETTERS TO W. G. WHITTAKER

GUSTAV HOLST

LETTERS TO W. G. WHITTAKER

Edited by
MICHAEL SHORT

With an introduction by
IMOGEN HOLST

UNIVERSITY OF GLASGOW
PRESS
1974

Printed in Great Britain by
T. & A. Constable Ltd., Edinburgh

CONTENTS

ILLUSTRATIONS

ACKNOWLEDGEMENTS

The texts of Holst's letters are reproduced by permission of the University Court of the University of Glasgow, and of the copyright owners, G. & I. Holst Ltd. Whittaker's letters are reproduced by permission of his Executor, Mr Edward Pollitzer.

The illustrations are reproduced by kind permission of the following:

1. Mr David Loeb (photograph by Sydney J. Loeb).
2. Mrs M. Pollitzer.
3. The Keeper of Portraits of the Royal College of Music.
4. The British Library Board, the publishers, Roberton Publications (for J. Curwen Ltd.), and the copyright owners, G. & I. Holst Ltd.
5. Miss Vally Lasker, and the artist, Miss Amy Kemp.

WILLIAM G. WHITTAKER

Born at Newcastle upon Tyne in 1876. After a general education, commenced the study of science, but subsequently changed to music, studying with local teachers. Appointed as an Instructor in music in the Department of Fine Art at Armstrong College, Newcastle upon Tyne, in 1898, becoming a Lecturer in the same department in 1920. Awarded the degree of Doctor of Music by the University of Durham in 1921. From 1913 was Assistant Conductor of the Newcastle and Gateshead Choral Union, and was appointed its Conductor in 1919. Founded the Newcastle Bach Choir in 1915, giving performances of Bach cantatas and various other works, including a three-day Bach festival in London in 1922 and performances of Byrd's 'Great' Service in 1924. In 1929 was appointed first Gardiner Professor of Music in the University of Glasgow and the following year also became Principal of the Scottish National Academy of Music. Served on several official music committees and gave series of lectures at various universities: also acted as an examiner for the Associated Board of the Royal Schools of Music, and became General Editor of the Oxford Choral Songs series. Works include piano, choral, and orchestral music, consisting of original compositions and arrangements of North-Country folk tunes, and also articles and books on music. Was awarded Carnegie prizes for his compositions *Among the Northumbrian Hills* and *A Lyke-Wake Dirge* in 1921 and 1924 respectively. Died in Orkney in 1944.

GUSTAV HOLST

Born 1874 at Cheltenham. Studied at the Royal College of Music from 1893 to 1898, subsequently earning his living as a trombone player until 1903 when he commenced teaching at James Allen's Girls' School in East Dulwich. In 1905 was appointed Director of Music at St Paul's Girls' School, Hammersmith, and in 1907 Director of Music at Morley College. From 1916 organised Whitsun festivals at Thaxted and elsewhere, and in 1918 went to Salonica under the auspices of the YMCA to organise musical activities among the troops there. In 1919 was appointed a professor at the Royal College of Music and also lecturer in music at University College, Reading. Visited the University of Michigan at Ann Arbor in 1923 to conduct his works at a music festival and made another visit to the USA in 1932 to conduct and lecture. Gave series of lectures in various places, including 'England and her Music' at the University of Liverpool in 1925 and the Cramb lectures at the University of Glasgow in 1928. Works include operatic, orchestral, choral, vocal, and instrumental music: although many were intended for amateur performers, they include masterpieces such as *The Planets*, *The Hymn of Jesus*, *The Perfect Fool*, *First Choral Symphony*, *Egdon Heath* and *Hammersmith*, which were to make him one of the major composers of the twentieth century. Died in London in 1934.

INTRODUCTION

By IMOGEN HOLST

THE first time I saw Whittaker was, I think, in 1913 when he came to our home at 10 The Terrace, Barnes. I was six, and he seemed to me to be immensely tall and energetic. I can remember my father's obvious delight at having him with us, and during the next few years I could recognise the particular excitement in his voice whenever he told us: 'Will is coming!' Later on, when I went to St Paul's Girls' School, I began to know Whittaker through his music, for my father taught us to sing his arrangements of 'North Countrie Ballads', insisting on the right pronunciation of 'Saw ye owt o' ma lad/Gan doon the waggon way?'

After my father's death, Whittaker wrote to me saying: 'I saw your letter in the press asking for correspondence of your father. The enclosed batch is very miscellaneous. Some of the things are of no importance, but I thought I had better send them. They are not in any chronological order as they have just been pushed into a file.'

I quoted from about twenty of the letters in my *Gustav Holst: a biography* (Oxford University Press, 1938; 1969). Since then, several extracts have become familiar owing to their appearance in articles on musical education and in essays on twentieth-century composers. For instance, there is his search for 'the musical idiom of the English language'; his description of harmony classes at Morley College ('we write rounds instead of counterpoint and spend the lesson in singing them'); his statement about criticism ('a sympathetic critic's disapproval is the most interesting and stimulating thing I know'); and his belief that 'music, being identical with heaven, isn't a thing of momentary thrills, or even hourly ones. It's a condition of eternity.'

A few years ago I learnt the good news that the complete collection of his letters to Whittaker is now safely housed in the Library of the University of Glasgow. When Michael Short suggested that the letters should be published, I felt doubtful at first. It was not because of the scrappiness of the brief notes giving information about times of trains. And it was not because of any unguarded references to other people. (I feel sure that the present relationship with his publishers will not be endangered by an occasional outburst such as 'Novello are sometimes awkward' or 'Stainer and Bell are blighters!') But it was the personal idiom of these written conversations that made me hesitate: the spelling of 'Nuf Ced' for 'enough said', and all those remarks about eggs. (Whittaker was a vegetarian and a teetotaller, which explains the admonition: 'Young man, you need a holiday: or beer: or meat: or something of the sort.') After thinking it over, I realised that my doubts were not worth bothering about, and I agreed that the correspondence should, if possible, be published as it stands.

The letters give a wonderfully clear impression of the way my father talked. Many of them must have been written in a hurry, and some of them show unmistakable signs of weariness. He led a 'double life', teaching on weekdays and composing on Sundays and during the month of August. There are frequent glimpses of the strain on his nervous energy: 'I suppose this term really *will* come to an end some day!'; 'How wonderful it is to have a free evening'; and 'Oh my friend, why do we waste our lives trying to teach! (Don't trouble to answer—I've already thought of several answers.)' Throughout his life he suffered, on and off, from neuritis in his right arm. It was in order to spare his painful hand that he sometimes sent dictated letters to his friends, apologising for the apparent formality.

The typewritten letters in this collection are the only ones that show the full date with the year. (Fortunately many of the scribbled notes are written on postcards, and the postmark is quite often legible.) Michael Short, with skilled editorial persistence, has aimed at discovering the right year for those of the undated letters that refer to concerts, because my father kept programmes and press notices of most of the performances of his works.

I am grateful to the University of Glasgow for allowing these possessions to be shared by readers who are unable to travel to Scotland to see the originals. The letters are what Whittaker himself described as 'a permanent record of a great man'. And they are a lasting proof of the debt that my father owed to those musicians who were his friends, a debt which he acknowledged when he wrote: 'I believe very strongly that we are largely the result of our surroundings and that we never do anything alone. Everything that is worth doing is the result of several minds playing on each other.'

EDITOR'S NOTE

THIS collection of letters exists as such simply because W. G. Whittaker took the trouble to keep most of the letters which Holst wrote to him over a period of many years. Although many of the items are of no great consequence and consist merely of such mundane matters as practical arrangements for forthcoming meetings, lectures and concerts, the whole collection is interesting as a record of the friendship between the two men, and as a source of insight into Holst's personality. As Imogen Holst has pointed out, these letters were written in the course of Holst's day-to-day musical life and were often hurriedly scribbled on the way from one teaching job to another, but although such circumstances clearly do not lend themselves to the formulation of weighty aesthetic diatribes for the benefit of posterity, the very haste of writing ensures a directness of communication which sometimes reveals the true nature of the writer and his artistic attitudes with surprising clarity.

Unfortunately, the collection as it stands is a rather incomplete record of the dialogue between Holst and Whittaker, as is understandable in a correspondence spreading over more than twenty years, but it is to Whittaker's credit that he made the effort to preserve as many letters as he could. Some letters which Holst probably wrote to him from Salonica during his war service there may never have reached their destination, and also, of course, at times when they were seeing each other frequently there was no need for written correspondence. However, in spite of these limitations, the letters provide one of the few sources for a deeper understanding of Holst the man and musician, and their publication as a collection is therefore amply justified.

Like all such collections, these letters give a one-sided view of the correspondence, and the reader must quite often guess at the content of the replies, but fortunately Holst did keep a few of Whittaker's letters to him, and these have been included in Appendix 4.

Because the letters were often written in haste, they do not always conform with the orderly arrangement one would expect to find in a published edition, and it has therefore been necessary to make some editorial amendments in preparation for publication. Holst hardly ever put the year at the head of his letters, often just writing the day and month, and in many cases he wrote simply the day of the week, e.g. 'Sunday', or sometimes nothing at all. Thus, in order to put the letters into a chronological sequence, dates have been assigned to them, using various kinds of evidence, both from the texts themselves and from other sources. In many cases this evidence is quite straightforward, consisting of postmarks on envelopes or mention of dateable events in the texts; in other cases approximate dates have been assigned by means of persistent detective work, while a certain number of letters has remained virtually undateable. In all cases, editorial additions to dates have been shown within square brackets, whatever their provenance, whether they have been obtained from clear postmarks (which do not necessarily represent the exact date or place of writing) or by guesswork.

Again, because of the haste of writing, the addresses are not always complete, and a list of the main addresses from which Holst wrote has therefore been given in Appendix 5.

As these were private letters between friends, Holst did not bother a great deal about layout or correct spelling and punctuation. In general, the amount of editorial alteration has been kept to a minimum, in order to keep as near to the original as possible, but some amendments have been necessary. For instance, postscripts sometimes appear above the beginning of a letter, or even on the outside of an envelope: these have been relegated to their proper position following the signature. Spelling and punctuation have been corrected where they are clearly wrong, but in cases where usage permits alternative versions, the original has been left unchanged, even though this has resulted in certain inconsistencies. Obvious slips of the pen have also been corrected; e.g. 'Could luck' for 'Good luck', and 'work' for 'walk', and very occasionally words have been inserted in square brackets in order to clarify the sense of a phrase.

Explanatory footnotes have been added to give details of works or people mentioned in the text, but again these have been kept to a minimum to avoid overloading the letters with annotations. Full details have generally been given on the first mention of a work or person, and thereafter only abbreviated information by way of reminder. All musical works referred to are by Holst, unless otherwise stated (except in the case of anonymous and traditional works). Although an attempt has been made to provide as much useful information as possible, several allusions remain rather obscure, and where there is doubt as to the person or work referred to, a footnote has generally not been given.

Finally, I would like to record my gratitude to Miss Imogen Holst for her kind help and advice during the preparation of these letters for publication, and also for providing much useful information from her own memories of the events concerned. Without her help the work on these letters would have been very much more difficult, but I should point out that the chronological sequence and the footnotes assigned to the letters are my own, and do not necessarily represent Miss Holst's views. I would also like to thank all the other individuals and organisations who have given me assistance in this work; especially Mrs Janis Hughes, Miss Vally Lasker, and the staffs of the Royal College of Music, the British Library, and the University of Glasgow.

LETTERS FROM HOLST TO
W. G. WHITTAKER

1

10 The Terrace,
Barnes, S.W.

April 22 [1913]

Dear Whittaker,

I would rather have a sympathetic conductor with no orchestra than vice versa. But the printed piano score errs in being a little too simple—I wanted it to be playable and sacrificed important details.[1]

The ideal plan would be for you to make alterations in the second piano part after consulting the score which latter I should be delighted to send you.

Perhaps however you would not have enough spare time to do so. If this could be done and if you could have a harmonium as well as the two pianos you could get a fine effect.

Page 35 of the piano score is quite another thing in the orchestral score—the orchestra are playing in about 12 parts, all high up and very soft.

Again, Page 21 is clumsy on one piano—it might be quite good on two. Anyhow I should be delighted to leave the matter in your hands. Let me know soon if you would like the score.

For 'a few voices' I suggest the first row of each part. For semi chorus who sing the 'message'—either a quartet or double quartet. The 'message' depends entirely on perfect declamation.

Good luck and many thanks for all the encouragement you give me.

Yrs Sincerely,

GVH

[1] This letter refers to *The Cloud Messenger*: ode for chorus and orchestra, op. 30. Although the original full score has been lost, the BBC Music Library has reconstructed it from a set of manuscript parts.

2

10 Lux: Gdn
Br Green

Sep 24 [1913]

Dear Whittaker,

Thanks for those copies which do me good to look at. My dear fellow you must do some more. 'Elsie'[1] is quite unique—everybody agrees that it is the finest thing of its kind going. Do send out a lot of specimen copies. I have a book of addresses—about 400—of conductors etc which I keep for sending Vedas etc. Would you like to have it?

B   I

Or better still—Stainer and Bell have the book now as they are sending out copies of my new things. Would you care to ask them to enclose a copy of one or all your folksong arrangements in every envelope except those obviously addressed to male voice or female voice choirs. Or leave it to their discretion. It would give me real pleasure if I could help in spreading the fame of Elsie and Co.

Yrs Ever,

GVH

[1] *Elsie Marley*: no. 2 of *North-Country Folk Tunes* arranged by Whittaker for unaccompanied mixed voices.

3

10 Luxemburg Gardens,
Brook Green, W.

Wed [1914]

Dear W,

Here's the music. Re the Purcell[1]—I enclose program.

Greig was soprano
Payne   „   „
Haselgrove was mezzo
Raggett   „   tenor
Poole   „   baritone
Hoare   „   bass

Nearly everything was put down a tone. You can see from this list how the solos are arranged. The parts are at your service but they are nearly all badly written although fairly correct. As regards the Vedas[2] I may discard or alter 'Dawn' and 'Aranyani'.

The Carols[3] are now published by Bayley and Ferguson in a cheap form—either mixed or female voices.

I hope you don't feel work as big a nuisance after last week as I do!

Yrs Ever,

GVH

Since writing I have gone through the program and put key and page of each number.

[1] The work referred to is probably *The Fairy Queen*, of which Holst had conducted the first performance since Purcell's time at Morley College in 1911.
[2] *Vedic Hymns* for voice and piano, op. 24 (originally entitled *Hymns from the Rig Veda*). *Aranyani* was not included in the final published version, and no trace of it now exists.
[3] *Four Old English Carols*, op. 20b (originally published by Arthur P. Schmidt in 1908).

4
St Paul's Girls' School,
Brook Green,
Hammersmith, W.

Dec 13 [1915]

Dear W,

I'm no good at teaching by correspondence but here are three suggestions.

1) Let me see yr next thing in its early stages.

2) Never write music when you feel excited.

3) Avoid jumping about from one key to another. The modern tendency is to enlarge the scope of a key—a very different thing. This is only the fringe of the matter but we <u>must</u> meet some time and then we'll have a good whack in. However these three points are sound as far as they go.

I had hoped that you might be coming up for the Music Conference here in Jan.[1] I'm down to speak on school orchestras and I wish I wasn't. It will probably do <u>me</u> good but I'm doubtful about the audience. Besides which I object to things doing me good in the Xmas holidays.

Yrs Ever,

GVH

Thanks for music.

[1] A vacation conference on musical education, held at St Paul's Girls' School from 3 to 8 January 1916 under the auspices of the Music Teachers' Association, the Home Music Study Union, the Girls' School Music Union and the Union of Directors of Music in Secondary Schools. Holst's talk on 'The School Orchestra' was reported in the *Music Student* for February 1916.

5
[Hammersmith,
London, W.]

[6 January 1916]

Sorry I haven't got a single one. Thanks for asking me all the same. I'm going to every meeting of this conference and feel ill in consequence!

Yrs,

GVH

6

10 Luxemburg Gardens,
Brook Green, W.

Feb 1 [1916]

Dear Whittaker,

Thanks for the new sources of pleasure you have sent me.

'Elsie'[1] created a storm of applause last night although the performance was not really a worthy one.

Yrs Ever,

GVH

[1] Whittaker's arrangement of *Elsie Marley*.

7

March 6 [1916]

Dear W,

So sorry for delay—I've been away at Cambridge.

We haven't got the Mozart—try Goodwin Tabb.

The 3rd Vedas[1] were written in 1910 for Frank Duckworth and his ladies' choir at Blackburn who were the first musical executants to take me seriously as a composer. I never saw them until 1913 when I went to conduct a programme of my own things but for about 12 years FD has always written and asked if I had anything for him to do and in the old days it used to buck me more than a little.

So Veda no III is an attempt at making a little return.

Am looking forward to the next Oriana.[2]

Yrs,

GVH

FD did Veda III (1st performance in 1911).[3]

[1] *Choral Hymns from the Rig Veda*: Third Group, for female voices and harp' op. 26 [no. 3]. The score carries the following dedication: 'This group is written for and dedicated to Frank Duckworth and his Ladies' Choir, Blackburn.'
[2] The Oriana Madrigal Society, founded in 1904 by Charles Kennedy Scott.
[3] 16 March 1911, at Blackburn Town Hall.

8

St Paul's Girls' School,
Brook Green,
Hammersmith, W.

March 30 [1916]

Dear Whittaker,

The sight of yr handwriting is always a joy but this last was the climax of many. My best thanks to you, your worthy pianist and your excellent choir. As for the unwarranted liberty you took with the last hymn[1] I shall put it into the next edition! Also I shall welcome any further suggestions.

About your visit to London. I want 4 consecutive hours of yr society preferably here. Is it possible? I had intended leaving town on Friday and returning on Monday in time for Morley in the evening. Shall you have any time free on Tuesday or would you rather rest that day?

Next Friday I have a farewell singsong at my Dulwich school[2] from 9 to 11 after which I am free until the 5 PM train.

Would you care to meet me at Dulwich and we would sample the picture gallery (which is adorable) ((also small)) (((also free))) and then we would come here.

If neither Friday or Tuesday will suit let me know and I won't go away. I've got heaps to show you and to play you and to talk your head [off] with.

If you care to hear my Dulwich girls sing be at the school by 10. It will be a rough unrehearsed go as you please sing song—not a lesson and certainly not a 'performance'.

It will be grand to see you again.

Yrs Ever,

G

[1] *Hymn of the Travellers*: no. 4 of the Third Group of *Choral Hymns from the Rig Veda*, op. 26 [no. 3]. See Whittaker's letter to Holst: Appendix 4 (c).
[2] James Allen's Girls' School, East Dulwich Grove, where Holst taught from 1903 to 1919.

9

St Paul's Girls' School,
Brook Green,
Hammersmith, W.

[31 March 1916]

I wrote my letter just after a visit to the dentist. Nuf ced! To begin with I forgot that you only arrive on Friday. Let me have a card about Tuesday—I can easily stop in town.

What is my May Day Carol?[1] As far as I know I have never written one. I feel very much inclined to arrange a folksong especially for the occasion in case there has been a mistake.

Yrs,

GVH

[1] Holst did in fact write a *May Day Carol*, for voice and two violins. A copy of the score is now in the Parry Room Library of the Royal College of Music.

10
Morley College
(For Working Men & Women),
Waterloo Road, S.E.

[April 1916]

Dear W,

There's some mistake. My Dulwich affair is on Friday next. I presume it is impossible for you.

Reserve Tuesday morning for me at St Paul's and I'll love you even more than usual if that is possible. I'll expect you at 10.30. Stop to lunch.

I'll have a try at doing a folksong for you as that carol[1] isn't a folksong at all!

Yrs in haste,

GVH

[1] The carol referred to was probably *This Have I Done for My True Love*, for unaccompanied mixed voices, op. 34. Although the words were taken from William Sandys' *Christmas Carols, Ancient and Modern* of 1833, the melody and harmonisation are entirely Holst's own.

11

Thursday [April 1916]

Dear W,

Just in case you are in London I write to say that my school is
James Allen's Girls' School,
E Dulwich Grove.

Take Tube (Bakerloo) from Regent's Park to Elephant and Castle (about 15 min) then get a policeman to put you into a tram going either to East Dulwich Station or Herne Hill, whichever comes first. (Either journey lasts 25 min.) Both are about 10 minutes walk from the school.

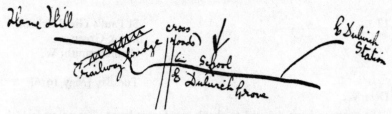

(I've got the railway bridge wrong—it should be in the dip of the road!) Don't let anyone send you to the Alleyn Boys School.

I shall leave there at 10.45 and if I don't hear from you (the school is on the phone) or see you I shall go to Thaxted and look forward to seeing you

a) Monday at 5 at the Oriana
b) Tuesday at 10.30 at SPG School
c) 　　,, 　　evening!

Yrs Ever,

GVH

12   Thaxted

April 24 [1916]

Dear W,

I like the two folksongs very much and will undertake to use at least 100 of both within 12 months of their publication. Also I think I can help to make them sell. I only wish I could play the piano parts—I'm afraid they will be a bit hard for incapable people like me to play when we want to give all our attention to the singers.

I hope I am not making matters worse by sending 'The Seeds of Love'.[1] I had given up all hope of writing anything for yr concert when this 'came' all at once just 24 hours ago along with some more ideas for arranging folksongs.

I forget when yr concert is—probably in a few days in which case it won't do any harm to send the 'Seeds' as you won't have time to do anything. I am very very sorry I could not do it sooner.

If there is time to do it please simplify or cut it in any way you like but don't worry over it too much.

Yrs Ever,

GVH

I return to London on Wed.

---

[1] *I Sowed the Seeds of Love*, which became the first of *Six Choral Folk-Songs* for unaccompanied mixed voices, op. 36[b]. The first three are inscribed: 'Dedicated to W. G. Whittaker and his singers' (see Plate 4).

13

St Paul's Girls' School,
Brook Green,
Hammersmith, W.

Tuesday [May 1916]

Dear W,

So sorry to have delayed to thank you for yr latest. I'm going to look through them when all this excitement is over—Whitsun and then Morley concert June 1st etc.

I don't know of any such flute as you want and our ♭ pitch flutes are very much wanted just now besides which they are modern fingering.[1] Try a tuning piece. I know it's not a real success but then it isn't by any means a real failure.

Yrs in haste,

GVH

[1] Presumably the flutes which Whittaker was using were tuned to the old high standard pitch, and he therefore wanted to obtain low pitch instruments which could be incorporated in a modern orchestra.

14

[Hammersmith,
London, W.]

[18 May 1916]

I suppose you knew that Edward Mason was killed in action last year. He did all the Vedas[1] and as the choir is disbanded his father is giving away the music. He consulted me and I suggested he should send some of the Vedas to you. I expect they will come next week. So glad you like the folksong. And am also glad I did it because I went on and did $4\frac{1}{2}$ more.[2] The $\frac{1}{2}$ being hung up until August.[3]

Hope your concert will be a huge success.

Yrs,

GVH

[1] *Choral Hymns from the Rig Veda*, op. 26. Mason had given the first performances of the Second and Third Groups in 1911 and 1912.
[2] Completed as *Six Choral Folk-Songs*, op. 36[b].
[3] August was Holst's only real free time for composition each year, being the only month free of teaching duties.

15   SPGS

Thursday [1 June 1916]

Dear W,

'Bonny'[1] ought to have gone better. It went correctly and smoothly but there was not enough light and shade. Perhaps it was because they had sung the Morley in a wild reckless manner and felt the need of playing for safety. 'Bobby'[2] went well considering the poverty of basses that we all suffer from. Act III of Dido went absolutely perfectly. Generally speaking it was a good concert but excepting for the above it was not thrilling.

How wonderful it is to have a free evening!

Hope you're going strong.

Yrs Ever,

GVH

Monday Just discovered that this has not been posted.

---

[1] *Bonny at Morn*: no. 11 of *North-Country Folk Tunes* arranged by Whittaker for unaccompanied mixed voices.
[2] *Bobby Shaftoe*: no. 8 of *North-Country Folk Tunes* arranged by Whittaker for unaccompanied mixed voices.

16

June 18 [1916]

Dear Whittaker,

Thanks again for all your good deeds. I would have written before but I was so tied up with our music festival (or rather feast) at Thaxted last week.

It was a feast—an orgy. Four whole days of perpetual singing and playing either properly arranged in the church or impromptu in various houses or still more impromptu in ploughed fields during thunderstorms or in the trains. It has been a revelation to me. And what it has revealed to me and what I shall never be able to persuade you is that quantity is more important than quality. We don't get enough. We practise stuff for a concert at which we do a thing once and get excited over it and then go off and do something else. Whereas on this occasion things were different. Take the Missa Brevis[1] for instance. The Morleyites had practised it since January. On June 3rd they did it twice through at their concert. On June 10th they rehearsed it and other things for three hours in Thaxted Church. On Whitsunday we did it during service in the morning, again in the evening, again on Monday morning. And some enthusiasts went through it again on Tuesday morning with violin and piano. The same applies to the other things we did. Some of the motets were learnt over a year ago.

In the intervals between services people drifted into church and sang more motets or played violin or cello etc. And between all this others caught bad colds through going long walks in the pouring rain singing folksongs and rounds the whole time. The effect on us was indescribable. We weren't merely excited—we were quite normal only rather more alive than usual.

Most people are overcome by mountain air at first. In the same way others are excited by certain big music. The remedy in both cases is to have more and more and More! What a mercy it is that we cannot meet otherwise I'd jaw your head off. I enclose the programme. There were about 15 Morleyites, 10 St Paul's girls, 10 outsiders and 10 Thaxted singers. The latter did grandly. Most of them work at a factory here and I have been asked to give them quicker music next year. It seems that they sang all day every day at their work for months and the slow notes of the Bach chorals seriously affected their output!

Yrs Ever,

GVH

[1] J. S. Bach's *Short Mass in A major*.

17   St Paul's Girls' School,
                                                Brook Green,
                                                Hammersmith, W.

                                                [7 July 1916]

Thanks for letter, MS and card. Good luck to the cottage!

Yrs Ever,

GVH

18   St Paul's Girls' School,
                                                Brook Green,
                                                Hammersmith, W.6.

                                                Oct 11 [1916]

Dear W,

You do know how to make people happy!

I'm going to stick to Mr Turnbull's letter and shall probably have it framed.

I should very much like to write to him or Mr Henderson.

That 'scrap of paper' is the greatest event of my life during the last 14 months.

Yrs Ever,

GVH

I send the Vedas.[1] I may want them back soon—could you copy any you particularly want to stick to?

I send you a song you may like—I'd forgotten all about it! Sorry I haven't a better copy.

[1] *Vedic Hymns* for voice and piano, op. 24 (originally entitled *Hymns from the Rig Veda*).

19
St Paul's Girls' School,
Brook Green,
Hammersmith, W.

Oct 23 [1916]

Dear W,

Write at once to

E Buttar Esq,
107 Elgin Cres,
Notting Hill,
London W.

and tell him exactly when and for how long you want the ♭ oboe.[1] (By the bye he has an oboe d'amore if you ever want one!)

He is the best amateur I know and is always most helpful.

You may also hear from a Mr Bonnett. If all else fails (but not before) post off enclosed and write to Wallace[2] yourself. You see I left the Scot Orch 16 years ago and although Wallace is a good chap still it is asking a good deal. So we'll only attack him if the others fail.

Let me know if I can help in any other way. (Only don't ask me for tenors—Morley choir started last month with 50 women and 2 men and 50 per cent of the men could not sing!) Max[3] was up on leave yesterday—he is a Bombardier now. Fine title isn't it?

Yrs Ever,

GVH

[1] i.e. low (modern standard) pitch oboe.
[2] J. E. Wallace, manager of the Scottish Orchestra.
[3] Holst's half-brother Matthias von Holst, the son of Adolf von Holst and his second wife Mary Stone.

20

Oct 25 [1916]

Dear W,

1) I'm telling Buttar to send the oboe d'am and save further bother. He has already started on the track of 2 other oboes!

2) Remember the d'am[1] transposes a 3d down—sometimes JSB forgets this as in the Xmas Oratorio.[2]

3) Send me circulars etc as I think I can get you subscribers—anyhow one or two.

4) Let me know if there's anything else you want.

Yrs,

GVH

P.S. I was sorry your French critic friend didn't write.

PPSS We're doing Handel's L'Allegro without tenors and my 2nd Vedas.[3]

[1] Oboe d'amore.
[2] This may be a reference to the custom of writing oboe d'amore parts in the alto clef.
[3] *Choral Hymns from the Rig Veda*: Second Group, for female voices and orchestra, op. 26 [no. 2].

21

St Paul's Girls' School,
Brook Green,
Hammersmith, W.

Nov 1 [1916]

Dear W,

I'd love to conduct the 2nd Vedas in March although I shall be in a blue funk over Agni.[1] Don't do the 'Swallow leaves'.[2] Either the East: Pic:[3] or the Pastoral[4] or one of the Princess songs[5] would be better. It would be jolly to hear the Ave Maria[6] again. Could you get two or three violinists and a tambourine for the Vedas?

Yr bandmaster certainly may score the Travellers[7] in—of course if he wants to publish it we must come to some arrangement.

I see you need a 2nd oboe—Buttar was on the track of another so write to him. I <u>may</u> know of a 3d! I accept offer of railway fare—will you put it into the funds of the Bach Choir[8]—I promised you some subscribers and this is no. 1.

Isn't the ob dam[9] a lovely creature?

Yrs Ever,

GVH

I suppose you wouldn't want the 2nd oboe for long?

[1] *To Agni*: no. 2 of the Second Group of *Choral Hymns from the Rig Veda*, op. 26 [no. 2].
[2] *The Swallow Leaves Her Nest*: part-song for unaccompanied female voices.
[3] *Two Eastern Pictures* for female voices and harp or piano.
[4] *Pastoral*: part-song for unaccompanied female voices.
[5] *Songs from 'The Princess'* for unaccompanied female voices, op. 20[a].
[6] *Ave Maria* for unaccompanied female voices, op. 9[b].
[7] *Hymn of the Travellers*: no. 4 of the Third Group of *Choral Hymns from the Rig Veda*, op. 26 [no. 3].
[8] Newcastle upon Tyne Bach Choir, founded by Whittaker.
[9] Oboe d'amore.

22
St Paul's Girls' School,
Brook Green,
Hammersmith, W.

[19 November 1916]

Just heard from my old Morleyite Norman Ramsden that he has sent his oboe to you. He has had consumption—I don't know if there is any danger of infection. Keep it as long as you like and return it to me if he has not put his address on it.

If you don't send a written promise to put my railway fare to the Bach Choir I shall take steps accordingly!

Yrs,

GVH

23
Morley College
(For Working Men and Women),
Waterloo Road, S.E.

Nov 20 [1916]

Get that oboe disinfected or at least consult a doctor. Ramsden has been in hospital for 2 years with consumption—he is getting better now I'm glad to say.
Also the oboe will want overhauling—it hasn't been used for 2 yrs.

Yrs,

GVH

24
St Paul's Girls' School,
Brook Green,
Hammersmith, W.

Nov 21 [1916]

Dear W,
Can't understand why ob hasn't come—perhaps it has by now. The owner's address is
Norman Ramsden,
Brompton Hospital Sanatorium,
Frimley, Surrey.
If it hasn't come write and tell him so. He has not seen it for nearly 2 years and wrote home for it to be sent to you. His people may have had trouble in finding it. Mind you have it disinfected. Keep it as long as you like. What is Gueritte's[1] address? I want him to come to my 'opera da camera' Savitri[2] on Dec 5.
It's exciting news about the Cloud.[3] But before deciding wait and see the new choral folksongs.[4]

Yrs,

GVH

Don't you think the Cloud needs rather a larger choir? I wonder!

[1] T. J. Gueritte, a French engineer working in Newcastle who was also interested in music and was secretary of the Société des Concerts Français.
[2] *Savitri*: an episode from the Mahabharata, op. 25.
[3] *The Cloud Messenger*, op. 30.
[4] *Six Choral Folk-Songs*, op. 36[b].

25
St Paul's Girls' School,
Brook Green,
Hammersmith, W.

Dec 10 [1916]

Dear W,

Thanks for oboe, letter and partsongs. My joy at the latter was a little dimmed by realising that they are not meant for schoolgirls—anyhow not for mine. But I hope to do them at Morley sooner or later. They are very jolly.

When you told me about your loss of subscribers I wrote to various people and amongst others to Balfour Gardiner.[1] The result was startling—he wants to help considerably but wants first to know the details of the whole thing. Of course I only meant him to write to any old great aunt or such like who happens to live in your part and to get her to subscribe. I'm explaining to him. Please forgive me and put all the blame on me if you don't want to go any further.

I think I shall send my little 'opera da camera' Savitri in for the Carnegie fund. It had a very nice reception last Tuesday.[2]

The 2d group of Vedas[3] are out of print and on behalf of S and B[4] I beseech you to wait while we urge the printers to a sense of duty.

I'm sending you two carols[5] for chorus with oboe and cello that the Oriana are doing—hope you like them.

Yrs Ever,

GVH

---

[1] Henry Balfour Gardiner, composer and concert promoter.
[2] The first performance had been given on 5 December 1916 at the Wellington Hall, St John's Wood, London, by the London School of Opera conducted by Hermann Grunebaum. Holst's application to the Carnegie United Kingdom Trust (if ever made) was apparently unsuccessful, as the work was eventually published by F. & B. Goodwin Ltd. The Trust did, however, subsequently accept *The Hymn of Jesus* for publication by Stainer & Bell Ltd. in the Carnegie Collection of British Music series.
[3] *Choral Hymns from the Rig Veda*: Second Group, op. 26 [no. 2].
[4] Stainer & Bell Ltd.
[5] *Terly Terlow* and *A Welcome Song*.

26

St Paul's Girls' School,
Brook Green,
Hammersmith, W.

Dec 19 [1916]

Dear W,

I fear it will be a little difficult to get away from Sat to Wed although it is tempting—very tempting.

Would the Monday do as well? If not I will make necessity my excuse and bow to the inevitable and stay till the Tuesday and incidentally look forward from now to having a howling good time with you.

So sorry I forgot to send the carols before.

Yrs Ever,

GVH

27

St Paul's Girls' School,
Brook Green,
Hammersmith, W.

Feb 4 [1917]

Dear W,

In Varuna[1] I beat 3 in a bar for pp 1.2.3. Then 2 in a bar for pp 4.5.6.7.8.

But for learning the notes at Morley I do all sorts of things—I find people are not really bothered at first beating notes and then beating beats.

In Agni[2] I want to beat 2 in a bar according to the dotted line. 5 is so jumpy and difficult to follow.

At the bottom of p 18 I beat 6.

Could you get a tambourine for Agni? It adds to the general excitement —I'll send the part if you tell me to.

An organ or harmonium playing the long bass notes would be good in the 3d hymn.[3]

I enclose Morley's latest effort. Bressey's song caused a sensation. He wrote it in his soldier's pocket book in a dug out in the firing line. He was able to get leave for the concert being in England wounded.

Coward is doing the Fairy Queen and has written about my parts.

My brother Max[4] was able to get leave for the concert. He has been

PLATE I. GUSTAV HOLST.

PLATE 2. WILLIAM GILLIES WHITTAKER.

transferred to the 'Bing Boys' otherwise the 'Kaiser's Own' otherwise the 31st Middlesex. He sends his love. So do I.

Yrs,

GVH

¹ *To Varuna*: no. 1 of the Second Group of *Choral Hymns from the Rig Veda*, op. 26 [no. 2].
² *To Agni*: no. 2 of the Second Group of *Choral Hymns from the Rig Veda*, op. 26 [no. 2].
³ *Funeral Chant*: no. 3 of the Second Group of *Choral Hymns from the Rig Veda*, op. 26 [no. 2].
⁴ Matthias von Holst.

28

St Paul's Girls' School,
Brook Green,
Hammersmith, W.

Feb 27 [1917]

Dear W,

It is at last dawning on me that I've got to travel to a far distant land in a few days and stand up in front of a lot of clever musicians who know the Vedas[1] far better than I do. The prospect is thrilling but gives me cause to tremble inwardly. I've even forgotten what you are doing! Also I want to know—

1) Is the concert in the evening and therefore requiring evening dress?
2) At what time is the Friday rehearsal?

If you use the gong in the last hymn[2] I would like it to be played out of sight. Could you use the pedals of an organ for this hymn?

Yrs Sincerely,

GVH

¹ *Choral Hymns from the Rig Veda*: Second Group, op. 26 [no. 2].
² *Funeral Chant*.

29

[West Kensington,
London, W.]

[3 March 1917]

I know just how you feel—composers should never be allowed to conduct their things! But cheer up—you know how mild I am. The 8.30 train you mention is 8.30 PM arriving 3 AM or so!

Please teacher may I take the 10 AM and risk it?

Yrs,
GVH

I'll return by the 10.47 PM.

30

St Paul's Girls' School,
Brook Green,
Hammersmith, W.

March 5 [1917]

Dear W,

Imogen has German measles! I understand that it is safe for me to travel for the next 10 days but that after that I shall be suspect for a while. But I don't think I ought to accept your kind hospitality unless yr little girls have had it. So may I leave it to you to arrange where I am to stop? And unless I hear from you I will take the 10 AM train and go straight to the Central Hall Westgate Rd when I arrive.

Yrs Ever,
GVH

31

Morley College
(For Working Men and Women),
Waterloo Road, S.E.

March 5 [1917]

The doctor says I am harmless for another 10 days at least. So do as you think fit with me when I arrive.

Yrs in haste,
GVH

By 'harmless' I mean that I cannot possibly infect anyone. Still—?

18

32

St Paul's Girls' School,
Brook Green,
Hammersmith, W.

March 6 [1917]

Card read. Will wait at station as directed. If weather is just bad and not unparliamentary adjectively a walk would be splendid.

Yrs,

G

33

St Paul's Girls' School, W.6.

March 13 [1917]

Dear Whittaker,

Please convey my warmest thanks to the ladies of your choir, to Miss Eckford, to Messrs Wall[1], Mark, Hardy and Miss Page and to Mr Murley for the enthusiasm and hard work they have shown and for the great artistic treat they have given me and their audience.

It has been a great time for me and one that I shall never forget.

I am sorry about the trouble about Varuna.[2] It was all my fault—or rather my misfortune—for not being as tall as you! And I am wondering if a severe course of physical exercises would enable me to grow a little taller before I come to Newcastle again. What do you think? I have never heard the Ave Maria and 'Tears'[3] so well sung before and as I had not heard the 'Ave' for sixteen years you can guess what a joy it was to me.

I always enjoy rehearsals more than concerts but I have rarely enjoyed a rehearsal as much as I did on Sunday morning.

As for your share of it all there is nothing adequate that I know of to be said.

Yrs Ever,

Gustav von Holst.

P.S. Don't thank Miss Eckford—I'm going to write to her myself—her playing is most beautiful.

PPS I shall bring a fountain pen next time!

---

[1] Alfred M. Wall, violinist and leader of various orchestras in Newcastle.
[2] *To Varuna*: no. 1 of the Second Group of *Choral Hymns from the Rig Veda*, op. 26 [no. 2].
[3] *Tears, Idle Tears*: no. 3 of *Songs from 'The Princess'*, op. 20[a].

34

St Paul's Girls' School,
Brook Green, W.6.
March 20 [1917]

Dear W,

You've probably done many preposterous things in your time but I hope nothing more so than thanking me for that week end. Lord save us, what an idea! Young man, you need a holiday: or beer: or meat: or something of the sort. You and everybody else who has been through the mill know what a source of inspiration it has been for me. I fear the choir letter was very bad—it was written at odd moments between lessons after the night journey.

I hope to send off all the stuff you ordered next week end. Meanwhile here are the voice and violin things.[1] This copy is for you to keep. Their proper order should be I III II or III I II—I'm not sure yet.

Yrs Ever,

GVH

I also send a critique of Savitri which please return.

[1] *Four Songs* for voice and violin, op. 35. Only three of the songs were completed at this date.

35

[30 March 1917]

Enclosed

PF score and parts of Military band Suite[1] (Will send full score if wanted)
4 'Planet' pieces for 2 pianos[2] (3 more not ready for sending)
Carols and 'Ale' song[3]
Messenger Parts[4]

> Blessings on you all (you won't see them in the parcel but they are there all the same).

GVH

[1] *Suite No. 1* or *Suite No. 2* for military band, op. 28 nos. 1 & 2.
[2] These were copies of Holst's own two-piano arrangements of movements from *The Planets* suite, op. 32, which were played by Nora Day and Vally Lasker at St Paul's Girls' School and elsewhere.
[3] *Bring Us In Good Ale*: chorus for unaccompanied mixed voices.
[4] *The Cloud Messenger*, op. 30.

36

St Paul's Girls' School,
Brook Green,
Hammersmith, W.

March 31 [1917]

Yesterday I sent off all the things you wanted of mine except the list of comp which shall come anon. Good holidays!

Yrs,

GVH

Address Thaxted, Dunmow, Essex.

37

St Paul's Girls' School,
Brook Green, W.6.

[29 April 1917]

Sorry for delay—had to get home to look up books for the date you want which is March 4 1913.[1]

I trust that not only will you be allowed but will be <u>ordered</u> to continue your present form of N.S.[2]

Yrs,

GVH

[1] The first performance of *The Cloud Messenger*, op. 30, which was given at the Queen's Hall, London, by the London Choral Society and the New Symphony Orchestra conducted by Holst.
[2] Non-combatant Service.

38

St Paul's Girls' School,
Brook Green,
Hammersmith, W.

May 7 [1917]

Dear W,

We'll see about Miss Lawton's piano.
I'm wildly excited about the Vedas in Paris.

And oh how I wish I could hear you and your dear people in the 'Cloud'!
This list is overdue—the writer got the measles!

Yrs in haste,

GVH

39
St Paul's Girls' School,
Brook Green, W.6.

May 17 [1917]

Dear W,

First about the piano. The very best way is to wait and look about for a
1st rate 2nd hand one—there are a few Bechsteins and Bluthners still
knocking about. This is only possible if Miss Lawton is not in a hurry.
Otherwise the only thing to do is to get a new Broadwood or Steinway—it
would have to be an upright at that price. If she can afford to wait we will
write round and discover what 2nd grands are going. Wonderful bargains
are still to be had only it is all chance.

I'm sorry that I forgot what I am to do about the Bach trumpets. I shall
be seeing my trumpeter Moore in a few weeks—would you let me know
exactly what I am to ask him?

Good luck to Saturday. You will all be very much in my thoughts and I
shall be with you in spirit. Give all the performers my best wishes and my
best thanks for all they have done and are doing.

And I hope the audience will express to you all I am incapable of doing.

I'm glad you like 'Venus' so much. I am sending two of the others—
Saturn and Uranus—and I particularly hope you'll like Saturn.

The last one Neptune is so ridiculous on the piano that I have arranged
it for organ duet.[1] Even then it isn't quite successful. The original is a
blend of flutes, muted strings and a hidden choir of female voices.

Once more, Good Luck to Saturday and for ever after!

Yrs,

GVH

---

[1] The manuscript of this unpublished arrangement is now in the Parry Room
Library of the Royal College of Music.

40

St Paul's Girls' School,
Brook Green, W.6.

May 23d [1917]

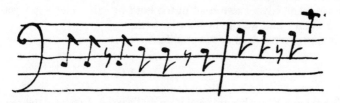

be unto you for evermore.

It's no good trying to thank you any more so I'll let JSB do it for me. And if any blighter considers the above blasphemous he either doesn't know

a) anything about religion or
b)   ,,   ,,   you   or
c)   ,,   ,,   both.

I enclose a billet doux for the tambouriniste[1] and am writing to Wall.

Now to answer questions. The old Invocation to the Dawn[2] was pretty bad but bears a family likeness to the first of the Veda songs[3] which was written long after. I think both the Pastoral and Welcome song were written about 6 years ago.

I am sending Saturn and Uranus today.

I'm greatly averse to fixed principles in art and I like everything—form melody harmony etc—to grow out of the original inspiration which latter is one of the mysteries and therefore quite unfit for polite conversation! I think a good rule is—'never compose anything unless the not composing of it becomes a positive nuisance to you.' Which is a paraphrase of what Samuel Butler said of learning.

But in case you want some padding for your lecture I find that un-consciously I have been drawn for years towards discovering the (or a) musical idiom of the English language. Never having managed to learn a foreign language, songs always meant to me a peg of words on which to hang a tune. The great awakening came on hearing the recits in Purcell's Dido. Can you or anyone tell me

1) how he managed straight away to write the only really musical idiom of the English language we have yet had

2) why he—who developed in every other way in music—never ever repeated this idiom (or hardly ever) but contented himself with more and more conventional recit secco in pure Italian style.

Well, I didn't get very far in Sita[4] which is good old Wagnerian bawling

I fear. But in all the Vedas[5] matters improved and in the CM[6] and Savitri[']
especially the latter, the words and music really grew together. Since then
I've managed now and then to do the same thing with other people's words
especially in the violin songs.[7] ('My Leman' is a good instance of a tune at
one with the words). But in all this there is no conscious principle, no
'ideal', no axe to grind. And I may do something quite different tomorrow.

Please thank Miss Lawton—I'm too busy to write. Her letter was just
what I wanted and we can now set to work.

Am very sorry indeed about yr wife.

Yrs Ever,
GVH

We are having another musical orgy at Thaxted. I enclose the morning
programme. The Byrd is the 3 part Mass. He lived near Thaxted.

[1] See Whittaker's letter to Holst: Appendix 4(d).
[2] No. 1 of *Six Songs* for baritone and piano, op. 15.
[3] *Vedic Hymns* for voice and piano, op. 24 (originally entitled *Hymns from the Rig Veda*).
[4] *Sita*: opera in three acts, op. 23.
[5] *Vedic Hymns*, op. 24, and the four groups of *Choral Hymns from the Rig Veda*, op. 26.
[6] *The Cloud Messenger*, op. 30.
[7] *Four Songs* for voice and violin, op. 35.

41
St Paul's Girls' School,
Brook Green, W.6.

June 4 [1917]

Dear W,

I enclose letter from Moore the Bach trumpeter. If you care to write to
him his address is

2 Foulser Road,
Tooting,
London S.W.17.

And now I want to try and write a little about Whitsuntide at Thaxted.
How I wish you could come and realise it for yourself in 1918. For it must
be realised. One of the advantages of being over 40 is that one begins to
learn the difference between knowing and realising.

I realise now why the bible insists on heaven being a place (I should call
it a condition) where people sing and go on Singing.

We kept it up at Thaxted about 14 hours a day. The reason why we
didn't do more is that we were not capable mentally or physically of
realising heaven any further.

Still as far as it went it was heaven. Just as the average amateur's way of using music as a sedative or stimulant is purgatory and the professional way of using music as a topic of conversation or as a means of money getting is hell.

Of course it's no use writing this. If you've had three days of perpetual music you've learnt it already if you haven't it's almost as sensible as describing the B minor to a deaf man.

Music—being identical with heaven—isn't a thing of momentary thrills or even hourly ones. It's a condition of eternity. As a girl in Thaxted said to me 'The great point of all this is that there is no reason why it should ever stop.' We had about 20 trebles 8 altos 2 tenors 3 basses 4 1st V 4 2nd 2 vlas 3 cellos one bass 2 fl 2 ob 1 horn 1 local cornet and organ. We rehearsed Sat 6 to 9. We did enclosed program on Sunday morning and Monday morning, rather a longer one on Sunday evening.

Both afternoons we did odds and ends in church—Morleyite compositions, rounds, canons (the 8 part one[1] in my 3d series with the 8 groups placed right round the church!) and also went round the village and serenaded people.

This was the official program. They filled in the intervals by singing and playing in church (where 'Sumer is icumen in' simply grew up from a group of people) in the houses, in gardens, on doorsteps (where I found 3 girls trying to sing the 8 pt round!) in the streets (the local policeman shut them up about 11 PM) and once on the church tower from whence they sang the Byrd Mass.

I arranged the three hymns[2] for choir and orchestra. The whole district is singing 'The Church bells in Thaxted' now—it is almost as popular there as Bach's Sleepers Wake.

Morley concert next Sat—Wesley's 'Sing aloud' Parry's 'Glories of our blood and state' Locke's Macbeth the 2nd Vedas[3] etc.

Yrs Ever,

GVH

You just come—my blessings on it and you and them. I hope it's all worth while. Don't know any one in Bournemouth but will see if others do.

Tell Miss Fleming to sing those songs as if she were saying her prayers and meant them!

---

[1] *Alleluiah* by William Hayes: no. 4 of the Third Set of *Sacred Rounds and Canons* by various composers, arranged by Holst for unaccompanied equal voices.

[2] *Three Festival Choruses* for mixed voices and orchestra, op. 36[a]. The original title of the third chorus *Our Church-Bells at Thaxted* was subsequently altered to *A Festival Chime*.

[3] *Choral Hymns from the Rig Veda*: Second Group, op. 26 [no. 2].

42
                                        St Paul's Girls' School,
                                        Brook Green, W.6.
                                        [5 June 1917]

Thanks for card. Have seen Mus Times.[1] Last night I learnt a fresh detail about Thaxted. A lot of Morleyites had to return home on Whitmonday night. As the train was crowded they were put into a horse box in which they sang 16th century motets all the way!
Vive Morley!

                          Yrs Ever,

                              GVH

[1] A brief review of Whittaker's performance of *The Cloud Messenger* was published in the *Musical Times* for June 1917.

43
                                        St Paul's Girls' School,
                                        Brook Green, W.6.

                                        June 27 [1917]
Dear W,

I know now what it is to be a spoilt child and it is all your fault. When I see your fist on an envelope I know that inside I shall find such kindness, good fellowship, self sacrifice and artistic insight that answering it as it should be answered becomes a sheer impossibility.

So instead of trying I'm going to pitch into you about the flea and the giraffe.

To begin with your simile is unfortunate as the flea is obviously mentally and physically superior to the giraffe.

But its the idea that one man should not criticise another whoever he may be that I object to. Of course you're a good critic—all artists must be as art implies selection. And a sympathetic critic's disapproval is the most interesting and stimulating experience I know. So many many thanks for remarks on Uranus and I hope for many more. Thanks also for the parcel of music.

I'm thinking of doing 'Bide with us' in the autumn and 'O Light ever-lasting' in the spring.[1] Any more suggestions?

We had a real bout of madrigal singing last Saturday. Seven Morleyites got the 3 part Morley and Weelkes and read one after the other hour after hour. It was good.

Would your Hindu friend be in London any time? We might have an evening together.

26

Would you mind indulging me in my weakness? If you will, would you let me know your exact birth time and place and those of the family?[2]

Yrs Ever,

GVH

[1] Bach's Cantatas no. 6 (*Bleib' bei uns, denn es will Abend werden*) and no. 34 (*O ewiges Feuer, O Ursprung der Liebe*).
[2] Holst was interested in astrology and sometimes cast horoscopes for his friends.

44   St Paul's Girls' School,
                                           Brook Green,
                                           Hammersmith, W.6.

July 9 [1917]

The cat is out of the bag! I am more speechless than ever and have suggested that Kennedy Scott should be approached and asked to supply the choral illustrations. Is yr birthday the 25th or 23d? And I want exact time, day, month, year, place. Sorry to be a bother.

Oh for holidays!

Yrs Ever,

GVH

Forgive me for referring to the flea again! I believe very strongly that we are largely the result of our surroundings and that we never do anything alone. Everything that is worth doing is the result of several minds playing on each other. To sponge on other people's ideas is the first duty of a composer. So if you refuse to criticise me the world will come to an end!

Yrs,

GVH

I learnt last Saturday how well bombs go with organ pedals! Does W[1] want the full score of the military suite?[2]

[1] James Causley Windram, Bandmaster of the First Battalion of the Royal Northumberland Fusiliers and dedicatee of Holst's *Suite No. 2* for military band, op. 28 no. 2.
[2] *Suite No. 1* or *Suite No. 2* for military band, op. 28 nos. 1 & 2.

45

St Paul's Girls' School,
Brook Green,
Hammersmith, W.

July 16 [1917]

CKS[1] would like to illustrate yr lecture but it depends on what you want of him. Could you do with just what the Oriana know of my things?— Carols, Eastern Pictures, Veda III.[2]

Yrs,

GVH

[1] Charles Kennedy Scott.
[2] *Choral Hymns from the Rig Veda*: Third Group, op. 26 [no. 3].

46

[West Kensington,
London, W.6.]

Sunday [22 July 1917]

Dear W,

CKS would prefer mid January for lecture. Would you write to him and fix a date and then we will settle with the Hall.[1]

He suggests doing female voice things and the Cornish Carol (Oh my love)[2] which latter he would do at his Xmas concert.

If you find that the whole affair would be too much bother of course you'll say so.

Bye the bye if they insist on having a chairman shall we ask R R Terry?[3] Don't forget to let me have birth times, and DO get a holiday!

Yrs Ever,

GVH

[1] The Royal Victoria Hall (the 'Old Vic'), where Morley College classes were held until 1924.
[2] *This Have I Done For My True Love*, op. 34.
[3] Richard R. Terry, director of music at Westminster Cathedral.

47   St Paul's Girls' School,
                                                        Brook Green, W.6.

                                                        Aug 1 [1917]
Dear W,

So sorry to hear about Mary.[1] Yr wife is having a rough time instead of the rest she should have.

I agree that the GVH lecture is an infernal nuisance and I wish we were strong minded enough to cancel it. Perhaps you are—I'm not!

CKS wants to do my Cornish carol at his Xmas concert and then repeat it at the lecture—I'm doubtful if it can be published in time. If it can't it would be nice if he'd do the folksongs[2] as they are dedicated to both of you.

However it's no business of mine. I'm trying to set the 'Hymn of Jesus' out of the Apocryphal Gospels for two mixed choirs, a 3d choir of female voices and an orchestra of rather more than a dozen, in other words, a damned big one. Incidentally I'm trying to learn Greek so as to read it in the original so altogether I'm very happy. Oh my friend why do we waste our lives trying to teach! (Don't trouble to answer—I've already thought of several answers.)

Thanks for your 'times'.[3] Am looking forward to a very interesting hour with them.

Good luck to the Trossachs.

                                                        Yrs Ever,

                                                        GVH

[1] Whittaker's daughter.
[2] *Six Choral Folk-Songs*, op. 36[b]. Nos. 4-6 are dedicated 'To C.K.S. and the Oriana.'
[3] The times and dates of birth of Whittaker and his family.

48   St Paul's Girls' School,
                                                        Brook Green,
                                                        Hammersmith, W.

                                                        [August 1917]

I've unearthed 'Horatius'[1] for your benefit (?). I'd rather you didn't show it to too many people. I may have been more than 12 when I wrote it. In fact I believe I was nearly 13!

It was the result of knowing Berlioz' 'Instrumentation' not wisely but too well and not knowing anything else about theory of music. I don't think I had ever learnt anything about a common chord although of course I knew the sound of one well enough.

I wrote it at odd moments in my bedroom etc until one sad day I took it to the piano and tried to play. I never wrote another note. Previously to that I had had it ringing in my head when walking (I was a good walker and an incessant one) but somehow what I played wasn't what I had heard in my imagination. Alas we've all been through that haven't we?

Yrs,

GVH

¹ The incomplete manuscript of this early cantata is now in the British Library. Whittaker had probably asked to see it in preparation for the lecture which he was to give on Holst's music.

49   Thaxted

Sep 1 [1917]

Dear W,

Have you and CKS settled on the date of the lecture? Because the Hall authorities will want to know. Give them a choice of Tuesdays if you can. I'm wondering if whether

1) it is not too early in Jan.

2) if you can arrive on the Friday afternoon before and rehearse that evening

3) if I can get them up to the scratch in time:—you would conduct some things of yours at the Morley concert on Saturday? I'm very doubtful. They will be raw and the Lord only knows what the tenors and basses will be like. Could you let me have a line about the date by Wednesday at St Pauls?

Yrs Ever,

GVH

50   St Paul's Girls' School,
                                         Brook Green, W.6.

Sep 7 [1917]

Thanks for letter. As the Hall people may want it put late I have sent in Jan 15 and 22nd as possible dates. What are your easiest things—or least hard? I thought of Hexhamshire Lass,[1] Sq Dacre[2] and Shoemakker.[3] But we might repeat Elsie Marley if you like. The trouble is that they are all beyond our powers! I want to do Bide with us. Could you lend us a score? (Of course not a Gesellschaft vol.)

Let me know later what solo illustrations you will want for your lecture. If they want a chairman shall we ask Terry?

Yrs,

GVH

[1] *The Hexhamshire Lass*: no. 9 of *North-Country Folk Tunes* arranged by Whittaker for unaccompanied mixed voices.

[2] *Noble Squire Dacre*: no. 12 of *North-Country Folk Tunes* arranged by Whittaker for unaccompanied mixed voices.

[3] *The Shoemakker*: North-Country folk song arranged by Whittaker for unaccompanied female voices.

51

Reid Bros., Ltd.,
28 Castle St.,
Oxford Circus, W.1.

Oct 3 [1917]

Dear W,

Sorry for delay—life has been exciting lately as you may have heard. The old extra large 28 size exists no more. Would either of these two do? If so write direct to above[1]—they have plenty of both. If not would you send the two samples back to them.

Yrs Ever,

GVH

P.S. Price 2/3 a quire.

PPS They find that they have only just enough for you and they will hold it back until you write.

[1] This letter was written on the headed notepaper of Reid Bros., Ltd., suppliers of music manuscript paper.

52

[Hammersmith,
London, W.6.]

Oct 22 [1917]

It should be Tam pia.[1]

We are getting on with the Hexhamshire lass. Should the last note of the first line in soprano be A or F? It is A in soprano and F in piano.

On page 3 it is C in both!

    ,,   ,, 5 ,, ,, F ,,   ,,

So sorry I have not heard about the date of lecture from the Victoria Hall people yet.

Yrs,

GVH

[1] Latin words from Holst's carol *Of One That Is So Fair and Bright* for un-accompanied mixed voices.

53   St Paul's Girls' School,
Brook Green,
Hammersmith, W.

Nov 6 [1917]

Hooray! Send her along. She'll be much too good for us and will probably forsake us for the Oriana after a bit but we'll keep her as long as she can stand us and—excepting when we sing worse than usually—we will make her happy. (Morley is a good place for the latter.)

Of course she could do both Oriana and us. Unless she prefers to join the harmony class at 7.30 just before the choir at 8.30. It's a very jolly one. We write rounds instead of counterpoint and spend the lessons in singing them. Of course she can write an oratorio if she prefers to. Morley is much nearer W. Norwood than the Oriana. No 68 bus (I think) will take her to the door.

They have definitely fixed Jan 15 for yr lecture unless you object. So we'll have the Morley concert on the Sat before (the 12th). Could you get up in time to rehearse on the Friday the 11th. And what would you care to do on Sunday—

to be left alone?

to have a 'birthday party'—which means about a dozen of us meeting and singing Weelkes and Morley madrigals?

or a scratch—probably scratchy—run through of my new thing for $2\frac{1}{2}$ choirs.[1] I'm doubtful about the possibility of this but it might come off.

Of course we don't mind if you prefer to get away from us for a few minutes—personally (and privately) I should sympathise as long as it is only for a few!

And now Miss Gray[2] is asking if you could not repeat the lecture on the Wed at school! What illustrations are you having? And do you want any

32

PLATE 3. Holst (*right*) and Whittaker (*left*), with James Oliver (conductor of the St Hilda band) and Edgar L. Bainton, at St James' Park, Newcastle upon Tyne, for the first performance of the *Two Psalms* on 18 July 1920.

PLATE 4. First page of the autograph score of *I Sowed the Seeds of Love*, showing the dedication to W. G. Whittaker and his singers.

PLATE 5. Christmas card sent to Vally Lasker in 1932, drawn by Amy Kemp, bearing the signatures of Holst, Whittaker and other musicians.

non-choral ones? Good luck to the two concerts. It will be 1st performances of my things.

But it is a disgrace to Newcastle to do you out of JSB.

Yrs Ever,

GVH

She <u>must</u> come next Monday—I'll explain to her why. I shall be at Morley at 6.30. Tell her to come early and take out a ticket—or come once without one to see if she can stand it and us.

[1] *The Hymn of Jesus*, op. 37.
[2] Frances Ralph Gray, High Mistress of St Paul's Girls' School from 1903 to 1927.

---

54   SPGS W6

Dec 1 [1917]

Dear W,

CKS tells me you've decided on the first two hymns of 3d set of Vedas[1] for Jan 15. I feel that those two alone would fall rather flat. He likes the second one. Would that one alone do and also 'Summer' from the Eastern Pictures? He does the latter extremely well. Also I've warned him that the Ave[2] is a nuisance to get up in a hurry.

Finally instead of no 1 of the four old carols[3] would you consent to 'Lullay my liking' which they did charmingly last year. Forgive me for bothering you so much. I'm writing in Thaxted. We're having a carol service in the dark tomorrow night!

Yrs Ever,

G

Remember Jan 15th is yr show. These are humble suggestions from a rank outsider who is not 'in it'.

[1] *Choral Hymns from the Rig Veda*: Third Group, op. 26 [no. 3].
[2] *Ave Maria*.
[3] *Four Old English Carols*, op. 20b.

55
[West Kensington,
London, W.6.]

Sunday [9 December 1917]

You seem to have come into the world solely to make people happy. Well, after all, that's only a roundabout way of saying you're a musician isn't it? Yr news is most thrilling and it's all your doing. The Pastoral is out of print. I've lent Scott all my copies—will you lend me 20 or 30 for the girls here? If so send them as soon as you can.

Yrs Ever,

GVH

56
St Paul's Girls' School,
Brook Green,
Hammersmith, W.

Dec 11 [1917]

I'll send the Mus: Stud: a copy. Please understand that I consider the 'Monster'[1] a wonder. It has all the defects of greatness but all the virtues also.

Could you spare or lend me a copy of the 'Northerner' with Scholes' article[2] on you? And may I quote largely from it in the Mag?

Yrs ever,

GVH

[1] *The Monster Book of Carols for Church and Home* (W. Scott, 1912).
[2] 'W. G. W.: a Londoner's Impressions' by Percy Scholes appeared in *The Northerner* (the magazine of Armstrong College, Newcastle) for March 1916, together with another article on Whittaker by R. C. Moles.

57
Tuesday [18 December 1917]

Dear W,

Last night the choir actually amounted to 52 including 12 men, 5 of whom were tenors. So I'm relieved to know that when you pull us to pieces on Jan 11 there will be something to pull. Squire Dacre[1] is grand. But the

Hexhamshire lass repeats are frantic and my attempts at explaining them give the choir hysterics. Do sing tenor in Bide with us and Weelkes' O all you lovely saints.

Balfour Gardiner's house 1 Hillsleigh Rd will be your residence. You'll be all alone but perhaps that will be a relief.

We will go through each other's things on either Saturday, Sunday, Monday or Tuesday mornings—or on each and every one. What time would suit you for the 11th (rehearsal)? I'll meet yr train and we will feed together. I wonder if you'd care to feed at Morley—it is primitive but rather nice.

On Sunday afternoon we will give you an un-birthday party of Madrigal singing. Would you please bring all your Weelkes? Re 'Tears'[2] CKS stipulated that the Oriana should be the only choir. If he does not do it I suppose he would not mind a double quartet of Morleyites doing it. Would you conduct them? So I'm not to be present on the 15th! I suppose you're right. I had intended disguising myself as a Bashi bazook or millionaire or musician and sitting at the back of the gallery. Is that forbidden? I'll ask Edith Clegg to sing the Vedas[3] (she was the first to do so in public) and the violin songs.

Miss Gray would love you to lecture here on the 16th. The obvious thing to do is the St Paul's Masque music[4] which is never allowed out of the school. But would you conduct it? I'd rather not have Tears it is too low for the girls but they could do the Pastoral and a couple of Planets and perhaps Edith Clegg would come.

The trouble is that the girls are hard at work on other things and school only begins on the 16th of Jan. Perhaps I could get them on the 15th—I'll try.

So glad to hear about the Bach Choir. I hope you'll start it properly next season.

Yrs Ever,

GVH

A great idea! Are you holidaying before the 11th? Could you come earlier and see Thaxted? But perhaps it will be too cold. Oh if you could be there at Whitsun.

[1] Whittaker's arrangement of *Noble Squire Dacre*.
[2] *Tears, Idle Tears*: no. 3 of *Songs from 'The Princess'*, op. 20[a].
[3] *Vedic Hymns*, op. 24.
[4] *The Vision of Dame Christian*: incidental music, op. 27a.

58   [Thaxted, Essex]

Dec 25 [1917]

The compliments of the season to you all and may the New Year bring
Peace and the boys home again. We had Bach, Pearsall, Byrd and others
this morning also cartloads of carols. Bring Weelkes Vols XI XII XIII to
London and tell Miss Rubin to keep Sunday afternoon Jan 13 free for
madrigals. Thanks for copies and programs etc. Vive le choeur de Bach!

Yrs,

GVH

59   The Steps,
                                                               Thaxted,
                                                               Dunmow.

Dec 31 [1917]

Dear W,

I've only got as far as the opening of your score—it is lovely and will
come off like fun. I'm going to examine the rest more carefully before
venturing an opinion. When you come to town do show me your settings
of carols. I particularly want to see the Chester Nun's one. I'm sorry to say
that the Weelkes singing on the 13th is 'off'. Would you tell Miss Rubin.

Another disappointment—I cannot meet you at the station on Friday
the 11th—at least not at 2. (I could do so any time after 4.)

So will you take the Inner Circle train to Notting Hill Gate station.
Hillsleigh Rd is 5 min walk from there. Could you arrange to have an early
meal so that I could call for you at 7.30?

Shall we go and see Terry on Sunday morning—it is his free time for
visitors after Mass. Our programme will be

Friday Morley 8.30 to 10

Saturday morning we'll have Whinnies and Carols and other North
Country fare—I'll come to Hillsleigh Rd.

Saturday afternoon?

More Whinnies?
or resting?
or talking?

or—best of all—you shall escape from me for a bit!

Saturday evening Morley 7.30 (no evening dress in Waterloo Rd!)

Sunday morning Westminster Cathedral.

The rest of Sunday? Another escape? (of course there's still the Gnostic Hymn![1])

Monday all day publishers etc (another escape!)

Monday evening more escape as I shall be at Morley

Tuesday morning St Paul's School. We want to inflict all the Planets on you.

Tuesday afternoon rehearsal for Wed afternoon lecture.

Tuesday evening 'Old Vic' lecture

Wednesday morning escape or Whinnies or Gnostic Hymn or what you will

Wed afternoon St Paul's lecture.

Wed evening escape—I'm at Morley.

I haven't a spare moment after that until Saturday so we will have a farewell tea together after the lecture.

Yrs Ever,

GVH

P.S. Clegg cannot sing on either the 15th or 16th. A pupil of mine with a light but small voice could do the violin songs and I might get someone else to do one or two Vedas on the Tuesday. Neither of them could come on the Wed I fear but I'll try. Would you sing 'Dawn'?[2] Or another? On the Wed you could have as many Planets as you please.

[1] *The Hymn of Jesus*, op. 37.
[2] *Ushas (Dawn)*: no. 1 of *Vedic Hymns*, op. 24.

60

Morley College
(For Working Men & Women),
Waterloo Road, S.E.

Jan 9 [1918]

Dear W,

At last I think I've got the solos fixed. At the last moment I've had to fall back on Morleyites but they will do them well in their humble way. Miss Lilian Twisleton will sing two Vedas—Varuna and Faith.[1]

Miss Dulcie Nutting will sing 2 violin songs 'My Leman' and 'I sing of a maid'[2] (I believe you don't know this one) violinist Miss May Blair (leader of the orchestra).

These with your Dawn should be enough. Wed's things Masque 15 minutes, Pastoral 3, 3 solo Vedas 12, 2 violin songs (if Dulcie can come)

about 6. Make it last about $1\frac{1}{4}$ hr or more. I've arranged not to be present at either lecture—I think it fairer on everyone.

Well, here's to Friday at 7.30.

Yrs,

GVH

¹ Songs from *Vedic Hymns*, op. 24.
² *My Leman Is So True* and *I Sing of a Maiden*: nos. 3 and 4 of *Four Songs* for voice and violin, op. 35.

61

Morley College
(For Working Men & Women),
Waterloo Road, S.E.

[23 January 1918]

Thanks for the gloves and chanties. But why has the Thermos flask returned? Sorry I did not make it clear that it was a present.

As I am not allowed to thank you for all the pleasure you gave us will you permit me to thank you for enjoying yourself so much? You see, it is a sure sign that you won all our hearts.

Yrs,

GVH

62

Morley College
(For Working Men & Women),
Waterloo Road, S.E.

[February 1918]

Dear W,

They want an analysis of the 'Cloud' at Liverpool. Forgive me! I've told them to ask you!

I am fed up with raids—in the day time the children are worn out and nervy and at night the cellar concerts are a great success but they last hours without any interval and leave one limp for tomorrow's work.

Yrs Ever,

GVH

63

Feb 26 [1918]

Dear W,

I send a) 21 vocal scores

b) some MS treble parts (after the trebles have had a look at the vocal scores these will be found quite useful).

c) full score for the sake of my pencil notes in tenor solo

d) organ part for soprano and viola aria

e) orchestral parts.

The wind are more or less as JSB wrote them excepting that the Cor Ang is arranged for clar and for fl 3 in cases of emergency. The string A parts are complete. I have added 'filling in' notes (see my score) to tenor air as I felt that the organ was unsuitable.

I have left final Choral without orch as I feel it should be done *pp* voices alone.

The violin B parts are lost. CDEF contain 1st chorus only but there are extra str parts to no V on separate sheets.

I hope this is clear. It's really not as absurd as it sounds and I send you the whole bundle of goods as nowadays one cannot be sure what will be useful and what not.

Morley marriages are usually sources of private woe to me as I lose pupils. But my best soprano Maud Smith has just married a 2nd violin Will Lewis. She brought him to the choir last night as a tenor (!) and he is making her learn the cello. Moreover the choir presented her with some money and she is spending it on buying an instrument.

Our opera[1] is postponed to March 9. We'll send details in time. I wish you were singing madrigals with us next Sat.

Yrs,

GVH

[1] *Opera as She is Wrote:* a parody 'in five scenes and six languages (including tonic sol-fa)'.

64

[c.12 March 1918]

Dear W,

I am returning the Northerner and also sending the Mag: containing (mis)information about last Saturday.[1]

It fulfilled my wildest dreams—that is everybody went away aching with laughter. I think I shall send you the Morley Early Victorian version of the

Keel Row—Adagio con molto espressione con molto coloratura con molto modulations—it's a scream. So was the Italian finale—3 soloists singing tonic solfa and the brigands shouting 'Away away she shall be mine' for 15 minutes. I was myself most upset by the French scene. But it was all good.

A fearful thing happened at Liverpool—they could not find the 'Cloud' timpani and perc parts. Have you got them?

I heard from an old pupil that the performance was extremely bad!

Yrs Ever,

GVH

May I have the 2 copies of 'Faith'?[2]

[1] *Opera as She is Wrote* was reviewed in the *Morley College Magazine* for March and April 1918.
[2] No. 9 of *Vedic Hymns*, op. 24.

65

[22 March 1918]

Many thanks for MS. Holidays are coming—hooroo! Although mine will be 'holidays' (?) because when one school ends another begins.

But we are all dreaming of Whitsun at Thaxted. Would that you could be with us.

Yrs Ever,

GVH

66

St Paul's Girls' School,
Brook Green,
Hammersmith, W.

[March 1918]

I'm sorry I know so little about the piano teaching at Wycombe Abbey. Strictly entre nous the next girl you have under these circumstances had better come here and I'll see that she gets on. My influence at Wycombe is slight.

Yrs Ever,

GVH

Fear there is little hope of a walk at Easter.

67

April 16 [1918]

Dear W,

Mr Louis Grein a Dutch merchant, a musical critic, a very good chap and a brother to J T Grein of the Sunday Times is writing to some friends in Scheveningen. He wants to know if EB[1] can travel in Holland.

We might run to about a doz copies of Dido. The London Bach Choir have some if you know Allen.[2]

Congrat: on concerts.

Hand is giving much bother so no more just yet.

Yrs,

GVH

[1] Edgar L. Bainton, composer and Principal of the Conservatory of Newcastle upon Tyne, who was interned in Germany during the war, being transferred to The Hague in 1918.

[2] Hugh P. Allen, conductor of the London Bach Choir and subsequently Director of the Royal College of Music and Professor of Music at Oxford.

68

[April 1918]

Dear W,

Mr Grein has sent this. Will you write to Bainton and tell him I'm so sorry I can't do so myself just yet.

Of course the introduction will include Dale[1] who, I hear, is in Holland —I shall speak to Grein about him. Grein knows all about both—also all about you and every one else worth knowing.

Yrs,

GVH

[1] Benjamin Dale, a composer who was also interned in Germany and transferred to Holland in 1918.

69

[Hammersmith,
London, W.6.]

[4 June 1918]

Xmas Day[1] can be done pf and str or any other combination but it's poor stuff anyhow and not worth doing.

41

Last Sat was quite good.

Congratulations on the BC[2] success. £30 worth of JSB at 4d each! Ye Gods!!

Yrs Ever,

GVH

[1] *Christmas Day*: choral fantasy on old carols, with accompaniment for orchestra or organ.
[2] Bach Choir.

70

[June 1918]

Dear W,

I hope you will find these Morley things[1] interesting, particularly the rounds—'Calcutta'[2] is amazingly effective.

We do the whole Masque[3] next month!

Yrs Ever,

GVH

[1] Compositions by Holst's pupils at Morley College. A selection of secular and sacred rounds chosen by Holst was subsequently published in the Oxford Choral Songs series (of which Whittaker was General Editor) under the title *Morley Rounds*.
[2] *There Was a Young Man of Calcutta* by Wilfred Palmer: no. 5 of *Morley Rounds*.
[3] *The Vision of Dame Christian*, op. 27a.

71

St Paul's Girls' School, W.6.

July 8 [1918]

Dear W,

I forgot to ask the Morleyites last Sat about their copies of Dido and now I shan't see them for ever so long. But I'll get one of them to see to it.

Scholes[1] has asked me to organise the music in Holland for the interned British soldiers under the YMCA so I may be away for a year. If you want to be even a bigger saint than usual do all my work here and at Morley for me during that time!

The Morleyites had a garden party here last Sat and I broke the news with disastrous results. However they cheered up under the influence of our spoof opera.[2] Then at the end came the most wonderful moment of my life. Everyone had been rolling about with laughter for over an hour and we were all dressed as brigands mermaids etc (I had just been Pelleas in a blue robe, a cork moustache and a yellow turban). As if it were the normal ending (probably it was) they all stood up as they were and sung the Byrd Kyrie as if their hearts were breaking.

I owe you a longer letter which I hope will arrive in due course.

Bye the bye Novello's publish some of the Dido choruses separately.

Yrs Ever,

GVH

If the affair comes off I go about August 15.

It's no good trying to thank you for the Herald[3] and all other things is it? But who is the 'Son of Sirach'?

[1] Percy Scholes.
[2] *Opera as She is Wrote.*
[3] An article entitled 'Mr G. von Holst', based on material supplied by Whittaker, had appeared in the *Musical Herald* for July 1918.

72   [Hammersmith,
                                            London, W.6.]

                                            [25 July 1918]

Not allowed to go to Holland because of my name.

Thaxted tomorrow! Rest!!

Then Composition!!! (or rather ???)

Yrs,

GVH

73   YMCA,
                                            Welbeck Camp,
                                            Notts.

                                            [September 1918]
Dear W,

Do any old thing you like with the 'Song' bless you!

I'm going with the YMCA to Salonica for a year—it is a special educational mission. In order to be of more use I am dropping my 'von'.[1] I'm here under canvas and in mud learning my job. I go home at the end of next week. If you'll be busy on the 29th it's no use inviting you to a special private performance of my Planets[2] that morning at Queen's Hall! Balfour[3] is treating me to it.

I shall probably go off in 3 or 4 weeks.

Yrs Ever,

GVH

[1] In order to avoid giving an impression that he was of German descent, although his family in fact came originally from Sweden, he dropped the 'von' from the name 'Gustav von Holst' when he commenced work with the YMCA among allied troops in 1918.
[2] This was in fact the first performance of the work, given by the New Queen's Hall Orchestra conducted by Adrian Boult.
[3] Henry Balfour Gardiner.

---

74   [France]

Nov 1 [1918]

After waiting 6 weeks I had to leave at 36 hours' notice.
My address will be

G T Holst,[1]
YMCA,
Piccadilly Circus,
Salonica.

The best of good luck to your fine efforts. Shall hope to write again when I get further on my way.

Yrs Ever,

GH

[1] His full baptismal name was Gustavus Theodore von Holst.

---

75   YMCA,
British Base,
Salonica.

Feb 4 [1919]

Dear W,

Thanks so much for your jolly letter. Now that demobilisation is setting in in earnest work here is rather erratic and uncertain. You journey 80 or

90 miles up to a camp and find that most of the men left three hours ago! It is all very right and very jolly so I don't mind.

I shall probably move to another centre before long where things and men are more stationary. Meanwhile I feel the most useful job I can do is to keep things going here as long as possible. For instance Colles[1] of the 'Times' started an orchestra at the Artillery School here. He left in November and now his deputy is leaving so I am carrying on. It is very jolly having a chance of doing Schubert's 'Unfinished' etc as an example for a lecture.

The rest of the work—lecturing, class teaching, organising—continues in spasms. Probably some effect is produced but it doesn't show on the surface because one gets a fresh lot of pupils every few weeks—sometimes days.

I hope you will be given a decent chance with the Choral Union.[2] Good luck to you and it.

And good luck and greetings to Bainton.[3] It is good to know he is back. How happy his wife must be. I have often thought of her and her pluck and faith and energy these four years.

I have met two Durham school inspectors—Cap Scott (Board of E) and Kirk (CC inspector). I'm hoping to see more of the latter when I get a move on.

Remember me to all good friends.

Yrs Ever,

GTH

[1] Henry C. Colles, music critic of *The Times*.
[2] Whittaker had been appointed conductor of the Newcastle and Gateshead Choral Union, having been assistant conductor for the previous six years.
[3] Edgar L. Bainton.

76
YMCA,
British Base Post Office,
Constantinople.

May 5 [1919]

Dear W,

You wrote me a letter that was stolen with all my kit the night I left Salonica. Now I have had your splendid one telling me of your Bacchic orgy.[1] Blessings and thanks as per usual. I've exhausted all my vocabulary on you and your singers long ago and I do wish I could express things a bit better.

Enclosed may interest you.[2] If it comes off it will be a lark won't it?

Work here is much more thrilling than at Salonica chiefly, I suppose, because I've now got some music to work with! It does make a difference. They want me to stay on another year and my bosom is rent in twain!

If you are doing strings and organ things at the Choral Union I wish you would look at my two Psalms for voices, strings and organ. Miss Day[3] or Miss Lasker[4] would send them to you from St Pauls. There are pf and full scores (MS).

I met an enthusiastic admirer of Ellis[5] the other day—an old Durham undergraduate who spoke his mind freely as to the relative abilities of Ellis and Culley. Sorry I've forgotten his name.

Yrs Ever,

GH

Stainer and Bell are blighters! I gave them the PF and str version of Dionysus[6] years ago!

[1] See Appendix 4(e).
[2] Probably the programme of Holst's forthcoming concert (see next letter).
[3] Nora Day.
[4] Vally Lasker, music teacher at St Paul's Girls' School, Morley College, and elsewhere. Made arrangements of several of Holst's works and helped him to write out his scores.
[5] William Ellis, organist of Newcastle Cathedral.
[6] *Hymn to Dionysus* for female voices and orchestra, op. 31 no. 2.

77   Constantinople.

June 16 [1919]

Dear W,

Thanks for yr jolly letter. Enclosed has nearly killed me but it's over now[1] and I sail for home tomorrow on 3 month's leave.

Shall   see   you in August
  „   bike   with „   „   „
  „   talk   „   „   „   „
  „   make music   „   „   „   „
Laus Deo.

Yrs,

G

[1] Holst had conducted a YMCA concert of British music given by massed choirs and orchestra at the Theatre Petits-Champs, Constantinople, on 9 June 1919.

78   On board ship

June 20 [1919]

Dear W,

I wrote a hurried line before leaving and now am going to answer your letter as it deserves.

The Hymn of Jesus has got the Carnegie prize.[1] My love to Kirk. My baptismal name was Gustavus Theodore.

Bless you, I never meant the Psalms for now but for any time during the next 20 years. And I fear Miss Lasker has sent you the Thaxted hymns[2] instead which is a pity. However there's plenty of time. I'm so glad you've got a decent vicar. That and Ellis (to whom endless greetings) ought to enable you to do big things. I wonder if you feel with me that music should either be done in a family party or in a church. I feel this more and more—it was Whitsuntide at Thaxted that convinced me first. One loses one's sense of individual personality and when that happens music begins. Anyhow them's my sentiments.

Let me know the exact time you come to town and when you want to cycle. I've smashed my bike! But we might walk or I might borrow one. I want to bring you to Thaxted and it would be jolly if we could cycle from there through Cambridge to Ashampstead. Anyhow we'll fix up a terrific time.

Yrs Ever,

GH

[1] It was published in the Carnegie Collection of British Music series by Stainer & Bell Ltd. on behalf of the Carnegie United Kingdom Trust.
[2] *Three Festival Choruses*, op. 36[a].

79

July 12 [1919]

Sir!

What the YMCA do you mean by suggesting such physical tortures? Balfour and I had planned a nice gentle fat middle aged tour for you— Thaxted, Cambridge, Oxford, Burford, Bibury, Ashampstead. And then you come along with your 600 miles record stunt! NO. I can't do it. I haven't a byke or the energy or the will.

And cuss your job on Aug 30. I'm conducting my Jap suite[1] at the Proms on Sep 1.

July 29th is St Paul's breaking up show. On the 30th my daughter will take me to Thaxted. You may come too if you promise to be good and mild and un-energetic. Otherwise let us have the evening of the 29th together and as much time as you can spare from Aug 14 to 28th.

Do just as you like about the trip. If you feel middle aged come with me. If you feel like WGW go with him!

I'm sending the Str Suite[2] and enclose formal letter about the Psalms. I wish you'd do 'Turn Back oh Man'[3] some day. It is really good. And the 'Church Bells of Thaxted'[4] must have fresh words. It is a really happy piece of music. Thanks for songs which I'm looking at tomorrow.

I'm having a wild time. My clothes were nearly torn off by 350 small people at my Dulwich school yesterday.

I'm at St Paul's early in each week and at Thaxted, Dunmow the rest. Either address finds me.

Yrs Ever,

G

I find that the 'Church Bells' was never sent to you. I am sending it with the Str Suite together with the Constantinople programme containing new words. If it were printed we would have the original words altered so as to be national instead of local.

Another delay! Will send Suite on Monday and Church Bells on Wed.

---

[1] *Japanese Suite* for orchestra, op. 33.
[2] *St Paul's Suite* for string orchestra with woodwind ad lib., op. 29.
[3] No. 2 of *Three Festival Choruses*, op. 36[a].
[4] *Our Church-Bells at Thaxted* (subsequently entitled *A Festival Chime*): no. 3 of *Three Festival Choruses*, op. 36[a]. It had been performed at Constantinople under the title *A Chime for the Home-Coming*.

---

80   Thaxted,
                                                     Dunmow.

                                                     July 16 [1919]

Dear W,

I asked Miss Lasker to send off the Str Suite but K Scott[1] wants the 'Churchbells' so they must wait. I will send off my beery carol[2] on Friday as I believe you have asked for it. Can I have the Str Suite[3] and the 2 Psalms as soon as possible? I want to get both in the hands of the printer soon. Goodwin and Tabb want the former and I thought of Curwen for the psalms. The Hymn of Jesus is to be done at the Phil next season.

Let me know your intentions re cycling and Thaxted and Ashampstead.

I am here Wed to Sunday and at St Pauls Monday to Wed each week this month.

Yrs Ever.

(*unsigned*)

[1] Charles Kennedy Scott.
[2] *Bring Us In Good Ale.*
[3] *St Paul's Suite*, op. 29.

81   Monday

[July 1919]

Dear W,

It might be better if you could come as soon as possible as we have an invalid coming to stay later on and it would be nice to have the place to ourselves. Could you travel up on Friday night and go straight to Liverpool Str

Liverpool Str		Thaxted
7.20 AM	arrives	9.34
10.5 ,,	,,	11.43

The drawback is that I have to catch the early train each Monday morning (I am in town Monday to Wednesday) so that would not give us much time. But it might fit in well with your cycling.

I suggest that you don't bring your cycle to Thaxted as there are plenty of nice places in walking distance. Just bring a handbag and leave everything else at King's X.

When you decide would you send a wire to 'Holst Thaxted'. When you come book to Elsenham—after that you have 6 miles on a light railway.

Longing to see you.

Yrs,

G

82   Thaxted.

July 19 [1919]

Dear W,

Thanks for 2 letters and scores.

Please do just as you like about cycling. If you follow out your original plan I promise I'll take care we meet a lot during your fortnight in town. On the other hand it would be very jolly if you could come here with us on the 30th for 2 or 3 nights and we would get in some walking but I would hate to spoil your tour.

E   49

If you came back by train would you care to spend a night or two with me at Ashampstead if Balfour invites us?

Let me know what you decide.

I have looked through the Psalms and I think that the best plan is to arrange the organ part for brass band. When we meet I want to ask you whether the wood wind should play with the voices throughout as there is so much unaccompanied singing. Then—if you like—you could put the wood wind amongst the singers to keep up the pitch. That is, if the pitch ever drops in your high latitude!

'Turn back' will probably be published along with the new version of the 'Churchbells' for the League of Arts so I fear I cannot put it with the Psalms.

Yrs Ever,

GH

83   Thaxted.

July 30 [1919]

Dear W,

Will you expect me at Cirencester station at 1.35 on Thursday the 7th? If either of us is not there the other will go to the Poste Restante to find out the reason why.

If I have to give up Cirencester I shall hope to meet you in Oxford on the 8th. In this case I shall let you know. The two best things in Cirencester are the 18th century park and the church—the latter is really fine.

If I fail to turn up see these two and then go on to Bibury, every inch of which is good. There is an inn on the riverside ('The Swan' I think) with a tea garden on an island which is quite good. If you have lots of time you might go up to Bourton on the Water. The New Inn there is good. Also if you want to talk to anyone find Cecil Wilkins or his brother John who are old pals of mine. But if you don't want to lengthen the journey go straight to Burford and stay at the Lamb. After Burford—which is glorious —get on to Oxford. Balfour expects us on the Tuesday.

Yrs Ever,

G

Yr card just came. I thought you did not require the Psalms until Easter! More of this when we meet. I see the word on your card is solfa—I thought it was Sep!

I'm writing to Augener's about it.

84

St Paul's Girls' School,
Brook Green,
Hammersmith, W.6.

[August 1919]

Thanks for yr letter. I am almost certain that I can come! It is chiefly a question of Monday's work and of fitting in trains.

Yrs,

GH

85

Sunday [August 1919]

Dear W,

If your latest postcard really means an invitation to give advice on piano tuning (I cannot make it read anything else) I must flatly decline.

Except when a note was more than $\frac{1}{2}$ tone out I always did more harm than good in my efforts.[1]

People should never experiment—it loosens the pins and makes the instrument infinitely worse in the long run.

If a piano is in a really bad way have it tuned twice in a fortnight. If it does not keep in tune after that probably the pins or wires want renewing.

I would willingly help in any way I can but in this matter I just know enough to know I know nothing!

Let me know if I can help in any other way.

Yrs Ever,

G

Am spoiling heaps of MS paper. If the fit continues I shall not come tomorrow.

---

[1] Holst had been provided with a set of piano repairing instruments for his work among the troops in Salonica and Constantinople.

86
                                                      St Paul's Girls' School,
                                                      Brook Green,
                                                      Hammersmith, W.

                                                      [18 October 1919]

I strongly advise you to give Nov:[1] a try.

                              Yrs,
                                G

[1] Novello & Co. Ltd.

87
                                                      St Paul's Girls' School,
                                                      Brook Green,
                                                      Hammersmith, W.

                                                      Nov 13 [1919]

Am getting score of str suite[1] from G and T.[2] Will send complete work to you on Monday. Nov:[3] have also returned my Hecuba.[4] A postcard is no place for expression of feeling as Nuf Ced.

                              Yrs,
                                G

[1] *St Paul's Suite*, op. 29.
[2] Goodwin & Tabb Ltd.
[3] Novello & Co. Ltd.
[4] *Hecuba's Lament* for contralto solo, chorus of female voices and orchestra, op. 31 no. 1; subsequently published by Stainer & Bell Ltd.

88
                                                      St Paul's Girls' School,
                                                      Brook Green,
                                                      Hammersmith, W.

                                                      Nov 20 [1919]

Suite going off tomorrow. Please excuse delay.

                              Yrs,
                                G

89
St Paul's Girls' School,
Brook Green,
Hammersmith, W.6.

Dec 22 [1919]

Dear Will,

I am deeply sorry for your disappointment. Forget all about it and have a good rest.

Will you be my guest anywhere, anytime anyday round about your lecture in London?

Yrs,
G

90
[early 1920]

Dear W,

This enclosed letter has been sent on.

You will please attend the Chinese Restaurant (vegetarian) Pic: Circus at 7.30 tomorrow to meet 1) Rodwell Jones who called on you years ago and to whom you were good, 2) his sister[1] a Morleyite, 3) Miss Lasker 4) ME. No. 3 is coming to the RCM for your answer.

Yrs,
G

[1] Mabel Rodwell Jones.

91
St Paul's Girls' School,
Brook Green,
Hammersmith, W.

Feb 1 [1920]

Dear W,

I've kept you waiting so long that I've almost lost all sense of shame so I'll cut apologies and come to business at once.

1) I did an unforgivable deed in carelessly sending one Xmas present to two young ladies. (Bye the bye I hope they like Phantastes.[1]) A bachelor uncle might have been forgiven but a married one never. The best plan will

be for me to repeat the dose and then let them each keep whichever one each prefers.

2) I liked your two first songs at the Oriana enormously. And I was struck by the contrast between them and your Scottish folksong settings which somehow seem to miss fire. And I wondered whether you had had rather too much of that sort of thing—one so easily gets into a groove and then one's work loses all its freshness.

3) And then I got your new batch of folksongs and quickly realised I was quite wrong!

But on mature deliberation I think I'm not altogether so. It is a limited form of art and you've done splendid work in it but when one works so long in a small form mannerisms are almost inevitable so I hope 1920 will produce a rich crop of original things from you and then any folksong settings you do afterwards will have a fresh outlook.

Anyhow that's how it strikes me.

I enclose last night's program. It was too short so we repeated the RVW. When that was over the audience still sat waiting for more and the only thing that made them budge was a speech from me!

When most of them had gone I turned on all the best readers (including yr Miss Rubin) to read the Kyrie of an alla Capella Mass that RVW is writing[2]—it is a glorious work. I think you would have liked their rendering of the Captain's Lady[3] although the altos were not strong enough for the last page—I added the 2nd trebles but that did not quite restore the balance.

Barring this question of balance the choir was really good and so was the band—not a single professional in it!

So glad to hear about New York and the publication of the songs.

Yrs Ever,

GH

Have you any vocal scores of Bach's 'Soul array thyself'? If so would you lend them to us until May 30? We could do with any number up to 40. Send them to Morley College Waterloo Rd SE1. (Must be English words). Also send any orch parts you have and can spare. Send me a card about this.

---

[1] George Macdonald's book *Phantastes: a faerie romance for men and women*, from which Holst had used extracts in some of his early compositions.

[2] Vaughan Williams' *Mass in G minor* for unaccompanied mixed voices, dedicated 'To Gustav Holst and his Whitsuntide Singers'.

[3] *The Captain's Lady*: Scottish folksong arranged by Whittaker for unaccompanied mixed voices (words by Robert Burns).

92   Thaxted.

March 7 [1920]

Dear W,

I owe you two letters!

1) If your folksongs insist on coming let'em all come! Never mind me or anyone else—write what comes. I'll try and write more fully during the holidays but the above is the real essential.

2) I'm a bit doubtful about coming to Newcastle in July. The journey is rather formidable and I'd have to forsake so much teaching or else travel by night neither of which prospect is very pleasing.

Needless to say, I should love to come—you know that don't you?

So may we leave it that 'I hope to come'? And then see how things are next term.

I've only just got the first proofs of the Psalms! If they are too late I strongly advise you to do Turn Back[1] and the Festival Chime[2] or 'All people'[3] which would sound fine out of doors.

The Psalms are scored for strings and brass—the latter might be doubled if the pitch agrees. As your choir is so vast would you care to put the wood wind among the chorus to support?

Yrs Ever,

GH

[1] *Turn Back, O Man*: no. 2 of *Three Festival Choruses*, op. 36[a].
[2] *A Festival Chime*: no. 3 of *Three Festival Choruses*, op. 36[a].
[3] Holst's arrangement of the 'Old Hundredth' for mixed voices and orchestra.

93

March 13 [1920]

Dear W,

Please convey my congratulations to the French Government for the honour you have done them.[1] I always understood they do this sort of thing better abroad.

For the rest Blessings as ever!

Yrs,

G

I'm still hoping for luck in July. How I wish the Psalms were at the end of the month! Then you'd take me a walking tour over the border wouldn't you?

[1] Whittaker had been made an Officier d'Académie by the French government for his work in performing French music in Newcastle.

94

St Paul's Girls' School,
Brook Green,
Hammersmith, W.6.

April 8 [1920]

Dear W,

It was very good to read about the Passion. 1000 Congratulations!

I'll send you the notices of the H of J.[1] It has made me realise the truth of 'Woe to you when all men speak well of you'.

I feel that something is wrong somewhere but don't know where or how.

The 1st ed is exhausted, the Phil is repeating it on June 2nd, the RCM and Oxford are doing it this summer and most other people in the autumn!

I hope you are getting a rest. It's a difficult thing to get nowadays isn't it?

Yrs Ever,

G

I've had a jolly letter from Windram.[2]

[1] *The Hymn of Jesus*, op. 37.
[2] James Causley Windram.

95

St Paul's Girls' School,
Brook Green,
Hammersmith, W.6.

April 26 [1920]

Dear W,

Certainly I would ask Balfour. If he doesn't want to come he'll say so (he does not love the North!) but in any case he will like being asked especially if you type the letter! Your script grows more wonderful each time.

Sorry I didn't send you the Te Deum[1] before. I also send the H of J cuttings which please return.

It is being repeated on June 2nd.

Yrs Ever,

G

[1] *Short Festival Te Deum* for mixed voices and orchestra.

96

[Hammersmith,
London, W.6.]

[14 June 1920]

I cannot possibly come on Friday. I can travel on Saturday morning and would be at your service in the evening. Under the circumstances don't you think I had better abandon the idea of conducting? I have no illusions about my powers in that line and a choir of that size is 'some' proposition.

Yrs,

G

97

St Paul's Girls' School,
Brook Green,
Hammersmith, W.6.

[21 June 1920]

Of course I'll conduct if I come but I wonder whether I should not wreck the show by doing so.

Anyhow I cannot start until Sat morn. Don't you think that that puts the lid on it? So sorry to disappoint you—and me!

Yrs ever,

GH

98

[Thaxted, Essex]

[26 June 1920]

Right oh! I'll conduct on the 18th and on the night before you must teach me the right tempi. The Psalms are scored for strings and brass. Would you like the woodwind to play with the chorus? Or to support the strings? Shall you conduct the Sop solo? Anyway give me a good lesson on my duties when I arrive.

Yes, RVW's article[1] is wonderful—and overwhelming. Yr competition must have been ditto! Thanks for program.

Yrs Ever,

GH

[1] Vaughan Williams' article 'Gustav Holst', published in *Music and Letters* for July and October 1920 and reprinted in his books *Some Thoughts on Beethoven's Choral Symphony, with writings on other musical subjects* (Oxford, 1953) and *National Music and other essays* (Oxford, 1963).

99

St Paul's Girls' School,
Brook Green,
Hammersmith, W.6.

[end of June 1920]

I find it absolutely impossible to stay over Monday. I'm so sorry!

As I'm not requiring any expenses except train etc do you think yr people would run to 1st class fare so that I could get a fairly decent night travelling on Sunday night?

I'm rather dreading it as I need a holiday like you and all of us.

Yrs,

GH

I'm writing to Augener about the brass parts.

100

July 13 [1920]

Dear W,

I thought that the wood wind should play from the vocal copies and therefore have not arranged them. There is no time now I fear.

They won't make much difference to the general effect either way and if the choir can sustain the pitch we could do without them.

Augeners have only just sent the proofs of the brass parts. I am sending them back at once—they were practically correct—with an urging letter.

But in case the parts don't reach you in time I now send you the original score of the brass parts so that parts can be copied if necessary.

Another idea strikes me—if your chorus keep the pitch and if your strings are not very good and numerous we will let the wood wind double

58

them. This can easily be arranged on Sat eve if you have a few spare string parts.

Yrs in haste,

GH

101

Sunday [August 1920]

Dear W,

The photos are splendid and the news in yr letter is damnable. Newcastle doesn't deserve you a bit and you ought to do work in London or somewhere and then people would realise what they had lost—perhaps they might even feel a little ashamed!

Failing that you ought to have a big choir once a week in some other northern city where you would be boomed. Otherwise we must just get you boosted—I wonder if Persevering Percy would take it on.

I cannot help hoping that if the C.U.[1] authorities turn out to be real swine, you will start a rival show and give free concerts in the Cathedral and get Clarke or someone to start a fund for orchestral and conductor's fees.

My dear boy, at the bottom of my heart I am the mildest of the mild but swine have thick skins and if you have to educate them it is necessary to use such means as will make some impression on them.

Nuf ced.

Yrs Ever,

G

[1] Choral Union.

102

St Paul's Girls' School,
Brook Green,
Hammersmith, W.6.

Aug 12 [1920]

Reading College[1] have decided to charge 5/- per member for the Choral Soc which has always been free before and they will give me ⅝ths of each 5/-. Is this idea feasible at Armstrong? It may not amount to much but it is

59

an honest attempt on their part to do the right thing. Balfour Gardiner is writing to you about a professorship at Johannesburg—£1100 to begin with! I almost think of trying myself.

Yrs in haste,

G

Just off to a Benedictine Monastery for a week where I am going to learn plainsong and write a comic opera.[2]

I'm going to arrange my string Suite (1st and last movements) for brass band.[3] Do you approve?

[1] Holst had been appointed lecturer in music at University College, Reading, in 1919.

[2] *The Perfect Fool*: opera in one act, op. 39.

[3] No trace of Holst's arrangements (if ever made) of these movements of the *St Paul's Suite* now exists, but the last movement of the Suite is itself an adaptation of the last movement of the *Suite No. 2* for military band which has been subsequently arranged for brass band by Sydney Herbert.

103

St Paul's Girls' School,
Brook Green,
Hammersmith, W.6.

[September 1920]

Dear W,

'Reader' at £150 does not sound good enough. It's just like you to be surprised at the feeling expressed. (Those people will be surprised if they ever learn my feelings towards Armstrong in general and Hadow[1] in particular!). Anyhow you'd better let everybody know that I am going to do my best to get you out of Newcastle because it's time you were treated as you deserve. The only thing to equal it was CVS's[2] treatment of RVW 25 yrs ago. Reichel has told me to send a bill for expenses to Major W P Wheldon DSO (Registrar) at the College. Reichel expresses regret about losing you. Bless you evermore for what you've done and are doing for the CM and Co.

Yrs Ever,

GH

[1] William H. Hadow, Principal of Armstrong College, Newcastle upon Tyne, from 1909 to 1919.

[2] Charles Villiers Stanford, Professor of Composition at the Royal College of Music, whose views rarely coincided with those of his pupil Ralph Vaughan Williams.

104

St Paul's Girls' School,
Brook Green,
Hammersmith, W.6.

Oct 5 [1920]

Dear W,

Bless you for them—they are really good and really <u>you</u>! 'Blow the wind'[1] is as good as 'Canny at Morn'.[2] And they are all three purely Choral which is what one looks for and loves in your work.

Thanks for the photos. My only consolation is that I must have afforded a little more or less innocent amusement to many a northern family circle.[3] But I didn't know I was quite as bad as <u>that</u>!

It is utterly impossible for me to come on Dec 1 which is a bitter blow because I don't want to hear or even think of the CM[4] until I hear it under you. I feel it belongs to you!

I thought of arranging the Jig only from my Str Suite[5] for brass band if you think it would do for yr competition. Would you ask someone the exact proportion of players for competitions? I forget one or two details.

We are doing some of the choruses from the B minor at Morley and I want Miss Rubin back! We have 40 rough sopranos who try and play follow my leader without a leader, ten altos who are really mezzos, ten good musical chaps who try and sing tenor (and who usually succeed!) and ten inefficient basses.

Next Sunday I am going to try and conduct some of the Planets at Birmingham with a band mostly composed of Cinema players. So you see, life is not dull. Also during the holidays I sketched the words and music of my comic opera on Parsifal.[6]

Yrs,

G

[1] *Blow the Wind Southerly*: North-Country folk-song arranged by Whittaker for unaccompanied mixed voices.
[2] i.e. Whittaker's setting of *Bonny at Morn*.
[3] See Plate 3.
[4] *The Cloud Messenger*, op. 30.
[5] *St Paul's Suite*, op. 29.
[6] *The Perfect Fool*, op. 39.

105

St Paul's Girls' School,
Brook Green,
Hammersmith, W.6.

Oct 11 [1920]

Dear W,

I am thoroughly ashamed of myself. In the hurry of getting off to Birmingham on Friday I forgot about your score and found it here on my arrival today. I have given it a fairly good look through and much as I should like to I dare not go through it again in case I lose the mail.

I enclose a list of suggestions. Since making it I have thought of another way of getting over the brass 'stodge'. Have one half of the bar horns *ff* and the other half trombones *ff*. There are several alternatives but do alter the place somehow. Never have stodgy *ff* brass and always remember that they sound 50 [times] louder to the audience than to conductor.

Do forgive me. I hope I have not put you into a hole through this delay.

Yrs,

G

Score coming by registered post.

106

St Paul's Girls' School,
Brook Green,
Hammersmith, W.6.

[17 October 1920]

Fear the Brass Band piece is impossible—I could not write anything of that length in time. Will keep list for reference. I hope the Greek chorus score[1] arrived in time. I've been longing to do my Perfect Fool opera for 14 years and at last it's begun. (N.B. It is meant to be funny.)

Yrs,

G

When you conduct at Aberdeen remember that brass sound 400 p. cent louder to the audience than they do to you.

Is it possible to buy those 3 photos? Everybody wants copies.

[1] Probably *Seven Choruses from the Alcestis of Euripides* for voices in unison, harp and three flutes.

107
St Paul's Girl's School,
Brook Green,
Hammersmith, W.6.

[25 October 1920]

Am sending orch parts I have. If you want any Bach parts from Germany I expect VL's sister in Berlin would be delighted to help you.

Yrs in haste,

G

Am only sending a few str parts but have many more also an extra score. Wire if latter is wanted.

I have also an organ part which you can have if you like only it is very bad.

108
St Paul's Girls' School,
Brook Green,
Hammersmith, W.6.

Nov 24 [1920]

Dear W,

Thanks for music and letter. How I wish I could hear you do the CM. I want to so much that I don't want to hear anyone else do it!

I enclose some cuttings. Please return. It was a real vulgar success! Holbrooke is getting deaf and I thought that Gueritte[1] might be able to help him a little. If so would you send the latter's address to

J. Holbrooke,
Harlech,
N. Wales.

So glad about Balfour. You really do inspire us! I'm snowed under with H of J proofs!

Yrs,

G

Good luck to Aberdeen.

You can have some Purcell any time. We have 3 suites and 3 oddments.[2]

---

[1] T. J. Gueritte.
[2] Holst arranged three suites of incidental music by Purcell for publication: *The Gordian Knot Untied*, *The Married Beau* and *The Virtuous Wife*. Among his surviving manuscripts is an incomplete arrangement of a suite entitled *The Old Bachelor*.

109

St Paul's Girls' School,
Brook Green,
Hammersmith, W.6.

Dec 3 [1920]

Dear W,

Would I could have been there! Amongst other more obvious reasons I should have swelled the numbers of the audience. You are a great man and you have brought the CM to life after it was half killed and entirely damned and you have done other wonderful things on my behalf but there is one thing that I doubt if even you could do and that is to teach me to forgive your city for its scandalous treatment and neglect of music and you (the two are synonyms as regards N on T[1]).

If you were in London or Birmingham or any other decent place!!

Yrs Ever,

G

Many many congratulations on Aberdeen.
You see what happens the moment you leave your benighted city!
I sent the 1st group of Vedas[2] before didn't I?

[1] Newcastle upon Tyne.
[2] *Choral Hymns from the Rig Veda*: First Group for mixed voices and orchestra, op. 26 [no. 1].

110

St Paul's Girls' School,
Brook Green,
Hammersmith, W.6.

[14 January 1921]

Why use the word 'dare'? Of course I'd love to come and I think I can as it is a weekend. The great problem is what to do with Friday's school. I dare say it can be wangled. Anyhow I'll have a try. Mind you come at Whitsun. The invitation means 1st cl fare + sleeping car both ways.

Yrs,

G

Sorry you've had such an awful time. I hope the invalids are better.

111
St Paul's Girls' School,
Brook Green,
Hammersmith, W.6.

Jan 31 [1921]

Dear W,

Hand bad so excuse brevity.

Thanks for choruses.

If you do H of J twice may I listen 1st time and conduct 2nd? Then may I skip all rehearsing in order to do all my Friday's teaching and catch the 5.30 train arriving at Newcastle at 11.11 PM on Friday?

May I return on Sunday by the 2.47 PM from Newcastle?

Yrs,

G

112
St Paul's Girls' School,
Brook Green,
Hammersmith, W.6.

Feb 4 [1921]

Dear W,

Righto—I obey. This time next month I'll be pretending to teach your good people something they know far better than I.

Miss Lasker wants to know which night you'll be staying at Talgarth Rd.

Also she bids me tell you that she has sent the cheque for the music to Berlin (£2).

Yrs,

G

I've no notes about the work. It is being done at Cambridge next Friday. If the prog is a good one I'll send you a copy.

113

April 3 [1921]

Dear W,

I rather wanted to be in Thaxted on the 14th and 15th. Is there any chance of yr coming on the 12th or 13th both of which would suit me beautifully. You know that VL[1] would love to put you up and I shall be free during the day time on both these days.

Arrangements for Whitsuntide are getting on. Whenever you like I will send you a cheque for return 3d class fares for

You
Lawton
Scott
Rubin
Middleton.

If any of them cannot come we beg that you yourself will revert to our previous wish and travel 1st sleeper.

VL will put you up. So far we have only fixed up for one other but I think I can manage the lot. You might ask the ladies if any of them have friends in town who would 'do' them.

I'll give you the music when we meet.

If you come to Hereford could you, RVW, and I have a mild tour—walking or biking—over the Malvern Hills afterwards? It would be grand.

So glad about Bournemouth—Bravo Dan[2]—he's a rare Bird!

Yrs Ever,

G

[1] Vally Lasker.
[2] Dan Godfrey, conductor of the Winter Gardens orchestra at Bournemouth.

114

April 27 [1921]

Dear W,

I understand that only Miss Rubin and Miss Middleton will be coming with you at Whitsun so the £15 should be ample for your comfort—if there are any trains at all!

VL will put you up. Probably the two girls will be put up near Isleworth. I suppose they don't mind.

You've got the Dioclesian chorus parts—as we hope you will be acting in the chorus that entails learning the thing by heart. I hope you don't mind.

p14 bar 2 note one in tenor should be B♮ not C.

p18 line 1 bar 5 note 2 in treble B♮ not B♯.

I wonder if you'll like it as much as I do!

I enclose music list for Sunday with treble parts of Burke's 'St Patrick'.[1] If you like we'll send complete sets for the girls.

Would you bring your overture when you come and leave it with me for a bit?

I rather think we shall have a great time and it's overwhelming to think that we shall have you.

Yrs,

GH

[1] *St Patrick's Prayer*: fantasia on Irish hymns, by Charles Burke, who studied at Morley College.

115

[Edinburgh]

[24 May 1921]

Hooray! Proudanappy to be Dedicatee.[1]

Yrs,

Gustav

[1] Whittaker had just received an award from the Carnegie United Kingdom Trust for his variations on an original theme for piano quintet, entitled *Among the Northumbrian Hills*. The work, which is dedicated to Holst, was published by Stainer & Bell Ltd. for the Carnegie Trust.

116

June 26 [1921]

Dear W,

Yr PF pieces[1] have been waiting on my table until I can go through them properly or, better still, get some one to play them. So far I've not had a minute for either so may I merely thank you for them and hope to begin to know them when this week is over.

Thanks for telling me about 'Turn Back'.[2] Those blighters never told me that it was put into solfa!

When I get a moment to spare I'll send my Greek choruses.[3]

I suppose this term really will come to an end some day!

Yrs Ever,

G

[1] Probably Whittaker's *Three Mood Pictures* for piano solo, published by Winthrop Rogers in 1921.
[2] *Turn Back, O Man*: no. 2 of *Three Festival Choruses*, op. 36[a].
[3] *Seven Choruses from the Alcestis of Euripides*.

117

July 18 [1921]

Dear W,

I hope the Doctorate[1] will make its due effect on your benighted Village and bring the good luck and comfort that is so long overdue.

I send Alkestis. I've strafed Augeners about the price which is a real shock to me.

Would you kindly correct enclosed proof of Turn Back in each $\frac{3}{2}$. The juggins has made it $\frac{6}{4}$! I feel that if you'll correct it, then and only then my mind will be at rest.

I'll lecture with pleasure—almost any Sat in the autumn is free so far.

Would 'The education of a composer'[2] do? I've done it in London and Edinburgh already. I suggest it because it is ready. I've ideas for a continuation called 'The teaching of composition'[3] but the other ought to come first. Or would you like me to damn exams for 90 minutes?

Yrs Ever,

G

[1] Whittaker had been awarded the degree of Doctor of Music at a Convocation of the University of Durham (of which Armstrong College was a part) on 28 June 1921.

[2] This lecture was subsequently published in *The Beacon* for October 1921 and reprinted in *Composer* No. 52 (Summer 1974).

[3] This was eventually entitled 'The Teaching of Art' and was published in *Heirs and Rebels* (Oxford, 1959) and the second edition of Imogen Holst's *The Music of Gustav Holst* (Oxford, 1968).

118

St Paul's Girls' School,
Brook Green,
Hammersmith, W.6.

July 28 [1921]

Many thanks for solfa. 'Ed of composer' is quite fit for a general audience. Have that if you want to be serious and Morley if you want a light entertainment. No hurry about date.

Get a good rest.

Yrs,

G

Just going to read the Music Student.[1] It looks good!

[1] An editorial article on Whittaker and his work was published in the *Music Student* for August 1921.

119   St Paul's Girls' School,
Brook Green,
Hammersmith, W.6.

Oct 2 [1921]

Dear W,

The books of songs[1] make a feast indeed. Thanks 1000 times. I have not heard the piano parts yet and have not even looked at them much yet because the tunes have fascinated me.

Would you allow me to murder two or three of them in a ballet[2] for Chicago? It sounds mixed but I got the books and a little commission from the USA about the same time and your tunes ran through my head when I thought of the ballet. But I shall ill-treat them disgracefully.

Don't trouble to acknowledge this. I know how busy you are.

Yrs,

G

[1] *North Countrie Ballads, Songs & Pipe-Tunes*, edited and arranged by Whittaker (Curwen, 1921).
[2] *The Lure* (scenario by Alice Barney).

120   St Paul's Girls' School,
Brook Green,
Hammersmith, W.6.

Oct 6 [1921]

Dear W,

Have I really treated you badly? I should be deeply sorry to think so but surely it is justifiable to postpone anything one knows will be a treat when things are more hectic than usual.

Besides starting term I've had Dioclesian (thanks to JMJ[1] it was splendid—the girl really has ideas), the Chicago ballet and the music for a big pageant.[2] I've got through most of it at the expense of my hand and after next week I hope to have one or two special pleasures amongst them a good

69

whack at your piano parts. I'll send out copies of songs later and VL will
send list of names for PF pieces.

Hope JSB arrived safely.

Yrs ever,

G

A Big Blow! We can only find a few Dioclesian chorus parts. We shan't
be able to send the rest until next week. I'm so sorry!

¹ Jane M. Joseph, one of Holst's pupils.
² *St Martin's Pageant*, performed at the church of St Martin-in-the-Fields,
London, by students from Morley College conducted by Holst.

121

[October 1921]

Dear W,

Sorry I was such an ass—was rather rushed at the time.

We found the Dioclesian copies and sent them off. But the pages are not
in proper order and the mistakes are not corrected. Later on we'll send you
some finished copies.

Could your people run to 30/- for hire of Dioclesian? It will wipe off
debt for paper etc.

The photos[1] are grand—bless you for them. But where are you? An
unknown or rather anonymous Person begs to invite you to London for the
Planets under Coates[2] on Nov 7. Also if possible for you, to stay for the
Tuesday Nov 8 performance of the Pageant for which I've arranged the
music. All exes found from door to door.

Any hope?

Yrs Ever,

G

¹ After a performance of *The Hymn of Jesus* at the Three Choirs Festival in
Hereford in September 1921, Holst, Whittaker and Ralph Vaughan Williams set off
on a walking tour of the surrounding countryside. Whittaker took several informal
photographs of the two composers, subsequently published in *Heirs and Rebels*
(Oxford, 1959) and *Ralph Vaughan Williams: a pictorial biography* (Oxford, 1971).
² Albert Coates.

122   Thaxted

Dec 28 [1921]

Thanks so much. I love de la Mare and look forward to a great treat. Vally has asked me about yr Sat show at the RCM. Will write you later when I've seen HPA.[1] How good holidays are.

Yrs ever,

G

[1] Hugh P. Allen.

123   Thaxted.

[January 1922]

Dear Will,

I wish I could be of more use but the truth is that I only know one cantata in each five you mention and of course I have not got the Gesellschaft.

Your programs look all right to me as far as I understand them and that is as far as I can go.

I think no one would object to JSB's bourrees and minuets in church—anyhow in London.

Ask someone else about an interval. If the concerts are short—under hour and a half—I'm against one. If they are longer then personally I prefer 10 to 15 minutes.

I've just had a jolly letter from Windram.[1]

The solo only of Süsser Trost[2] is published in English.

I will try and 'educate'[3] you on Feb 4 and shall expect you to do the same to me on Feb 5 minus the inverted commas. I will travel on Sat by the usual train. Will my expenses permit of a sleeper on Sunday night?

Yrs Ever,

G

Back in town on Monday.

[1] James Causley Windram.
[2] Bach's Cantata no. 151.
[3] i.e. Holst's lecture entitled 'The Education of a Composer'.

124
St Paul's Girls' School,
Brook Green,
Hammersmith, W.6.

[February 1922]

Dear Will,

Thanks so much for the photo. Although V[1] has commandeered it I see it oftener than you would expect. Both photos are excellent. I hope you agree to my suggestions re two oboes and a flute in that Bach cantata instead of 3 ob.

I am sorry you are having 3 trumpets—do you realise how resonant the Aeolian Hall is? For timp I strongly advise you to have Jane Joseph. She plays them excellently.

Do you want any more Dioclesian parts? Don't answer if you don't! Would you be able to lend us all the Dioclesian music from March 25 till April 10? I've promised to lecture to the ISM on Purcell on April 8.[2]

Yrs Ever,

G

Thanks for JSB concerto.

[1] Vally Lasker.
[2] Reports of this lecture to the Incorporated Society of Musicians appeared in *The Times* for 10 April and the *Musical Times* for May 1922. An edited version entitled 'Henry Purcell: the dramatic composer of England' was published in *The Heritage of Music*, volume 1, edited by Hubert J. Foss (Oxford, 1927).

125
Bournemouth

April 21 [1922]

I wrote you a card undertaking to judge essay and composition but lost it. Anyhow I will. I've had 2½ days cycling or walking in Dorset including a visit to Thomas Hardy.

Yrs,

G

126

[July 1922]

Dear Will,

I'm so sorry. I never made a note of my visit to Newcastle and have now forgotten all about it. Is it Nov 11?

Thanks for the Byrd. I don't think much of these ones but I expect he has some better ones.

I'm asking Novello to send you a copy of my Ode.[1] Don't show it to people until it is public property which will be some time in Sep. They want to prevent anyone doing it before Leeds.

Only 2½ weeks of term left!

Yrs Ever,

G

If you ever want a mezzo who can sing Bach and other things that sound like music remember

Joan Elwes,
Royal College of Music, SW.

[1] *Ode to Death* for chorus and orchestra, op. 38, first performed at Leeds Town Hall on 6 October 1922.

127

July 25 [1922]

Dear Will,

I'm a bit puzzled about Nov 11. If it is an invitation to listen I might be able to accept it but if I'm to conduct it means travelling on Wed and losing two or three days' work and you know what that means.

It was wrong of me not to make a note of the date when you asked me—I have no recollection of it whatsoever. I hope Novello sent the copy.

School concert today—Imogen plays the C♯ major book one of the 48 also plays 2nd horn in the orch (we are 50 now!) and gets a sight reading prize.

And tomorrow I get on the old bike and lose myself!

Yrs Ever,

G

128   [Hammersmith,
                                                  London, W.6.]

                                                  [18 August 1922]

Why I imagined that Nov 11 was a Thursday I don't know! I can easily
manage the Sat and will come on the Friday (the 10) in time for the
rehearsal.

Sorry to have given you so much bother.

Yrs Ever,

G

129

Aug 19 [1922]

Dear Will,

They've printed str parts and will print wind ones if there is enough
demand.[1] At present the latter are MS on hire.

Suite no. 2 will be out in a fortnight.[2]

I've just written a Fugal Ballet in strict Sonata Form.[3]

I'm getting Academic!

Yrs Ever,

G

[1] This probably refers to the *Ode to Death*, op. 38.
[2] *Suite No. 2* for military band, op. 28 no. 2.
[3] *A Fugal Overture* for orchestra, op. 40 no. 1.

130   St Paul's Girls' School,
                                                  Brook Green,
                                                  Hammersmith, W.6.

                                                  Oct 5th, 1922

Dear Will,

I will do the article on Purcell[1] unless they want it in a hurry. Tell
them to let me know when they want it. The Ode[2] is not arranged for piano
and strings but the orchestral string parts are published and these with a
piano ought to be quite satisfactory.

Sorry I shan't see you at Leeds. I am going there tonight and am looking forward to the Bach Concert tomorrow morning. The Perfect Fool was tried over here last Saturday morning. Clive Carey, Stuart Wilson and Mrs Southam sang and Vally played. I think it will be good fun.

November 10th will be our half-term holiday here so it will be quite easy for me to get off.

Yours ever,

Gustav

[1] This essay, based on Holst's lectures on Purcell, was published in *The Heritage of Music*, volume 1, edited by Hubert J. Foss (Oxford, 1927).
[2] *Ode to Death*, op. 38, which Holst conducted in Newcastle on 11 November 1922.

131

[Hammersmith, London, W.6]

[6 November 1922]

I'll take the earlier train on Friday—I shall be spending Thursday night with Bairstow[1] at York.

Am looking forward to another taste of the North.

Yrs,

G

Must leave on Sunday afternoon—perhaps even morning.

[1] Edward C. Bairstow, organist of York Minster.

132

St Paul's Girls' School, Brook Green, Hammersmith, W.

Nov. 17th, 1922

Dear Will,

The shirt is mine. Would you kindly send it to me by post. I am sorry to say that I have felt obliged to write to Halifax asking them whether I may send Vaughan Williams or Dunhill[1] or somebody like that as a deputy. I feel I ought never to have accepted the work as I am feeling rather tired and have the Planets at Birmingham facing me as well as many other little trifles. Of course they may keep me to my engagement but I earnestly hope

75

they won't. I am glad to see from the papers that even Newcastle people are beginning to realise what the Bach Choir means to the city.

Yours ever,

Gustav

Excuse dictated letter—it looks so jolly formal. I feel an awful ass over Halifax. How I wish I had your strength!

[1] Thomas F. Dunhill, composer and writer on music.

133

32 Gunterstone Road, Barons Court, W.14.

Dec 19 [1922]

Dear Will,

So sorry I cannot take on anything for May. America is not settled but it is more than probable.[1]

For easy madrigals I suggest

Come to me grief (5 pt) Byrd

Awake mine eyes (4 pt)   „

Say dainty dames 5 pt Weelkes

To shorten Winters' sadness 5 pt   „

Term is over!

Vally sends love.

So do I.

Happy Xmas.

Yrs Ever,

Gustav
(or what remains of him)

[1] Holst had been invited to conduct some of his works at a musical festival held by the University of Michigan at Ann Arbor in 1923.

134

Thaxted.

Dec 28 [1922]

Dear W,

Thanks a thousand times. It is good to have those two songs which I have loved since you first sang them to me. By the bye although I have often heard them since I have never heard them so well interpreted.

Thanks too for the books. The Family is devouring Newcastle while Masefield has prevented me from writing letters all day! Nuf Ced.

I'm having quite a good time. I'm not even pretending to walk or cycle and am eating and drinking hugely and have just upset a large bottle of ink most of which went on the carpet and the rest on other things including this paper and me.

Last night I was acting in charades—a curate holding a dancing class in a teetotal night club. Conrad Noel[1] was a performing lion.

Such is life—in Thaxted at Xmas. Good luck to you in 1923.

Yrs Ever,

G

[1] Vicar of Thaxted.

135
32 Gunterstone Road,
Barons Court, W.14.

March 26 [1923]

Dear Will,

The Missus is working hard so I'm answering yr letter. I'm getting on but feel strongly disinclined for work (Not that I do any!).

I'm off to Thaxted on Thursday and—all being well—shall come up on Sat April 7 for the day to hear RVW's Mass at Queen's Hall[1] at 3. I've got a ticket for you. Will you be my guest for lunch at 1 at Eustace Miles or—better still—will you meet my train at Liverpool St at 10.8 AM (train from Elsenham)?

I'm sorry I can't do what you ask but I've made a strict rule never to be patron or vice pres etc etc to anything or anybody.

Forgive me!

Yrs Ever,

G

[1] This was the first concert performance in London of Vaughan Williams' *Mass in G minor*.

136   Thaxted

Ap 4 [1923]

Dear Will,

1) Sorry not to be home to welcome you
2) „ the house does not look more welcoming and that the music
room is unusable.

3) The electric lights are quite helpful but get Vally to explain them as
they are puzzling at first—also the front door won't alway shut when
expected to so don't let it take liberties with you.

4) Will you come to 32 G on Friday at 4.30 and have high tea with RVW
and me?

5) Love to your Hostess
6) And to you.

Yrs,

G

137   Red Star Line.
                                                   On board S.S. Belgenland.

June 19 [1923]

Dear Will,

We hope to be home within three days after having had a very good time
in the USA.

And now to business—

We were guests of the state university of Michigan at Ann Arbor a
beautiful little town about an hour's train ride from Detroit and six hours
from Chicago.

There were suggestions that I should accept the post of professor of
music. It is a tempting one as there is a glorious chance of work amongst
1100 eager raw students with delightful people to work with but I don't
think I shall accept partly because I'm not up to the work (10 years ago
I'd have jumped at it) and partly because Imogen is not old enough either
to be transplanted or left alone in England. I have suggested you and
amongst other details I have told them a) that you probably would not
accept it b) that you will be passing through the USA at Xmas.

The present conductor of the choral society is a nice young chap called
Earl V. Moore. I am sending him copies of 'Bonny at Morn' and other nice
things of yours. Nothing is decided but

a) he may put your things into rehearsal in October

b) you may be invited to stay at Ann Arbor for a week or so and conduct them as you pass through the USA.

c) you may be sounded about the possibility of accepting the professorship.

My advice is, don't worry about (c) at present—anything may happen—I might even accept it myself which seems at present impossible or they may get someone else or (and probably) you wouldn't consider it for a moment.

But if they invite you to visit them I do beg you to accept even if it means curtailing your time elsewhere and postponing your return for a week or two. A week or so in Ann Arbor is worth a month rushing about. The people are not only kind but intelligently kind and without fussing you in the least they will give you one of the happiest times of your life.

I could write reams about Ann Arbor but prefer you to find it out for yourself. If they invite you the letter will be sent to you c/o Fritz Hart.[1] Probably it will come from Moore the conductor, Charles Sink the secretary or Dr Kelsie the president of the music society—all three equally nice, equally American and entirely different.

I enclose letters of introduction to Stock[2] the conductor of the Chicago orchestra, to Austin Lidbury of Niagara Falls and to Cecil Forsyth of New York.

Stock is a fine musician but a dreadfully busy man. Also Chicago is quite a place to avoid unless you've time to get to know it well.

Lidbury is head of some chemical works at Niagara. His family come from Lancashire and he has kept the real feeling for music. However busy he may be at times he makes time to see musicians and to entertain them. He's the greatest thing in Niagara—the Rapids are second, the power stations third, Lidbury's cellar fourth, the country around fifth and the Falls the twentieth.

Forsyth is an old RCM fellow who composes and writes books. I like him and he would be helpful but he is a rum bird.

My advice is, don't go out of your way to see Stock or Forsyth unless you've got plenty of time but if you go to Niagara or near it <u>don't miss Lidbury</u>. Remember that letters take a long time in the USA—people either use the telephone or telegraph. Lidbury knows your works so if you suddenly arrive there just ring him up and tell him I've told you to. He did Ca' Hawkie[3] last season. He has no more address than Lidbury, Niagara Falls, NY. If you had more time in the USA I could make more suggestions. I hope you've got plenty of copies of your things with you. One thing I've learnt that is important—choirs with mixed voices are not numerous as people prefer men's glee clubs and women's choirs.

I hope you are having a good time and that you will see much of dear old Fritz. Keep in touch with him as the Ann Arbor letter, if it comes, will be sent to Melbourne.

Love to Fritz and Family. And if you see the Mackails and Angela remember me to them warmly.

Yrs Ever,

Gustav

A good hotel in New York is the Netherland—corner of 5th Avenue and 59th Street. Of course they'd put you up in Ann Arbor.

[1] Composer and writer. At the Royal College of Music he was a fellow-student of Holst, and wrote the words for some of his early works. He became Director of the Conservatory of Music in Melbourne, Australia.

[2] Frederick A. Stock.

[3] *Ca' Hawkie Through the Watter*: no. 13 of *North-Country Folk Tunes*, arranged by Whittaker for unaccompanied mixed voices.

138

St Paul's Girls' School,
Brook Green,
Hammersmith, W.

Dec 23 [1923]

Dear W,

Thanks for jolly letter. What a term it's been! I've had 5 shows at QH[1] a lot of teaching at the RCM and huge classes here, Dulwich[2] and Morley.

Don't be shocked at either the price or the cover of this. Piano scores can be hired and you can easily get rid of the hideous Super Hun title page and use the inside page as cover.

Blessings and the Season's Greetings!

Yrs,

G

PS Enclosed is the 'Xmas Card' I am sending to Morley and others.
PPS Sorry! I haven't one left!!

[1] Queen's Hall, London.

[2] James Allen's Girls' School, East Dulwich Grove.

139

St Paul's Girls' School,
Brook Green,
Hammersmith, W.6.

Jan 28th, 1924

Dear Will,

Once again welcome home! I hope the journey round the world has really done you good and given you an occasional rest. It is good to know that we may see you this weekend but both Mary and Vally seem a little vague as to when I shall be allowed to see you. In fact Mary is rather more than vague and is, I think, counting on having you as her exclusive property during your few hours in London and I don't blame her. She has quite won our hearts and I cordially endorse Imogen's verdict "Mary is a dear". With regard to next weekend, I have the whole of Friday clear at present and probably Saturday morning also. On Saturday evening we have a Morley College Concert (Christmas Oratorio and other things) and I shall be free again on Sunday. Don't trouble to write but you might arrange with Vally and Mary that I am allowed to see you when you can be spared. I am so glad you had that good time with Lidbury who is a splendid fellow. I know little about Ann Arbor now so cannot tell you any news.

Yours ever,

Gustav

Since writing I have seen your last letter to Vally. It would be nice to have you at Morley on Sat but you are not to think of it if you have a chance of being alone with Clarrie and Mary.[1]

PS Just a word in strict confidence about myself. In some ways life is much easier for me. A rich man[2] after seeing the 'Fool' gave me a large sum of money and I have cut down my teaching by half and now lead a wonderfully lazy life—probably I spend as much time in bed or on the sofa in a week as you do in a month.

But it hasn't been an entire success. I have a longing to be by myself or with not more than one or two people at a time and I dread parties or business meetings etc. And I have a fear lest people shall imagine that success has spoilt me and that old acquaintances and old surroundings are not good enough for me. (Please note that I mean people and not friends.)

I'm giving up Morley in the summer and have dreams of going away to a hot place alone next winter.

But please don't think I'm grumbling. All this retirement has its good side. Since August I've sketched a long choral symphony[3] which anyhow is as good if not better than my previous best. So I'm a lucky chap and I know it.

---

[1] Whittaker's wife and daughter.
[2] Claude Johnson, a director of Rolls-Royce Ltd.
[3] *First Choral Symphony* for soprano solo, chorus and orchestra, op. 41.

140

32 Gunterstone Road,
Barons Court, W.14.

Thursday [February 1924]

Dear Will,

This is a horrible blow. My head got queer on Monday and worse on Tuesday.[1] In order to get fit for tomorrow I sent a deputy to the RCM yesterday and spent most of the day dozing by the fire and lying in bed. But it was of no use and I realise now that my presence in Newcastle would be a greater disappointment and inconvenience than my absence. Also I should be fit for nothing for the following week at least. Not that it matters for it may happen anyhow. But I daren't run any more risks over this silly business.

What I feel most is not hearing the CM. I had looked forward to it so much and you have done so much for the work that I look on it as your property.

And I do hate letting you down like this after all you've done and been to me. I'm going to indulge in Silence, Solitude and Heat (not mere warmth) and in my waking intervals I shall think of my three dear good people Will, Vally and Nora having a good time together.

Yrs Ever,

Gustav.

[1] Holst had had an accident to his head in 1923, while conducting at University College, Reading.

141

32 Gunterstone Road,
Barons Court, W.14.

Friday [February 1924]

Dear Will,

This is to wish you all three the greatest happiness and success. Greetings to Wall[1] Bainton[2] choir and orchestra (and BMS[3]—I'd prepared a fresh joke for my speech!).

Yrs Ever,

Gustav

[1] Alfred M. Wall.
[2] Edgar L. Bainton.
[3] The British Music Society, which held meetings and concerts in various provincial centres, including Newcastle upon Tyne.

142   Thaxted.

                                                  Monday [April 1924]

Dear W,

Thanks for letter and congratulations on the Carnegie award.[1] I am particularly delighted because I think it is your best work. I suppose you won't spend a night with me here when you come south? If you do I'll teach you to be lazy—it will be a new experience for you and will probably give you a shock. I've forgotten what work feels like! Don't trouble to answer this—if you find that you can come send me a wire at the last moment. But it's too much to expect.

                                                  Yrs Ever,

                                                  G

[1] Whittaker received an award from the Carnegie United Kingdom Trust in April 1924 for his *A Lyke-Wake Dirge* for chorus and orchestra.

143   Morley College
                                                  (For Working Men & Women),
                                                  Waterloo Road, S.E.1.

                                                  May 15 [1924]

Dear W,

A select body of Paulinas, Morleyites and other desirable beings feel that Whitsuntide will be so incomplete without you that they desire to humbly beg your presence at Dulwich from May 22 at 2.30 PM until May 24th at 9 PM. All expenses up to £20 will be paid!

Or failing this, could you come part of the time?

I haven't much hope but still one never knows!

I believe you've seen the program—it's chiefly Byrd!

                                                  Yrs,

                                                  G

144

Thaxted,
Dunmow.
July 6 [1924]

Dear Will,

Your letter reminds me that I never acknowledged yr 3 two-part songs for which I am

a) sorry because it was rude and

b) glad   ,,   the delay is making me realise my error in not liking them at first. I'm still a bit doubtful but I'm getting on and by Xmas I hope to be liking them very much. I wish I could hear them well sung. They are certainly original which is a great point. Certainly you have my permission (and blessing) to make use of the PF[1] for brass band comp. I'm sorry it's to be a selection which I loath—having played more than a few in my days—such things hang like a curse round brass band music. I suppose the ballet (Vally's separate piano version[2]) would hardly suit.

Of course you'll have to ask Novello who are sometimes awkward—I'll put in a word.

A brass band publisher came to see me last year and I begged him to consider arranging some Purcell since when I've not seen either him or my Purcell volume I lent him.

If my hand were only stronger I'd do the Purcell and perhaps even the PF myself but as things are I think I'd better keep off everything but original work. (I've longed for years to arrange certain JSB fugues for both brass and military bands.[3])

Barring my hand I'm having a lovely time. I lead the combined lives of a Real Composer and a Tame Cat!

Good luck to the holidays.

Yrs,

G

I once wrote a selection myself!—it was from Baring Gould's 'Songs of the West'.[4] Goodwin and Tabb have the score but I could get it any time you wished if your br band people would care to look at it. It would suit them better than the PF I fancy. Also I hope I could improve it a little before it was arranged—as far as I can remember it was only bad in places!

---

[1] *The Perfect Fool*, op. 39.

[2] Vally Lasker's arrangement of the ballet music from *The Perfect Fool* for piano solo (published by Novello & Co. Ltd.).

[3] In 1928 Holst arranged the *Fugue in G minor* from Book 3 of Bach's organ works for military band (and also for orchestra) under the title *Fugue à la Gigue*.

[4] In 1906 Holst arranged some West-Country folk-songs for orchestra, under the title *Two Selections of Folk-Songs*, op. 21. The following year he revised the work and made two works from it: *Songs of the West*, op. 21[a], and *A Somerset Rhapsody*, op. 21[b]. The manuscripts of these arrangements are now in the British Library and the Parry Room Library of the Royal College of Music, but there is no trace of the proposed arrangement for brass band.

145   32 Gunterstone Rd,
                                                                W.14.

                                                                Sep 7 [1924]

Dear Will,

This is my first day with a type writer so you know what to expect.

For many years I have tried to write a piano piece for Mrs O'Neill and this summer I have at last succeeded. And I finished it just in time to send it with an appropriate dedication to her on her silver wedding. But from another point of view it would have been more fitting to have dedicated it to you for it is a Toccata based on 'Newburn Lads'. In the first variation I seem to have 'sincerely flattered' you for which I ask your permission and your pardon. At the end I have 'flattered' the first man who ever played it to me. He was an old man in Cheltenham with a hurdygurdy somewhere about 1879 and this was his only tune and each time he played it he had fewer notes than before and what notes were left were further from what they were when they were young.

This has been the only blank August as regards composing that I can remember but it does not matter after my wonderful Spring and although I haven't really begun anything fresh I feel that it is just waiting round the corner. How about you? I hope that I may congratulate you on having 'spoilt music paper' in grand style and that your cottage has proved 'The Right Place' as usual.

Anyhow I can congratulate you on the BMS article.[1] It is rare that one gets a well written, appreciative and yet critical article. Bravo Foss.

I suppose you are full of great plans for the autumn. Whatever they are they are sure to be good so Good Luck to them and to you.

After recording St Paul's Suite[2] last week I have decided not to appear in public this winter and, if possible, do no teaching. When I start work again (or if I do) I want it to be really good which it certainly is not at present.

Meanwhile I am spoiling music paper to a vast extent and look to my gramophone royalties to keep me from bankruptcy.

I hope to see the final proofs of my Choral Symphony tomorrow. Novello has it and Curwen the Toccata. I have arranged my choral folk-songs[3] for male voices (except The Tree in the Wood[4] which won't go).

And as critics have decided that I can't write a libretto, the words of my new opera[5] have been written by Shakespeare. The sketch is nearly finished. So have I.

Yours Ever,

Gustav

[1] An article on Whittaker by Hubert J. Foss had appeared in the August issue of the *Music Bulletin* (the journal of the British Music Society).

[2] Issued on Columbia L 1648-9 (78 r.p.m. recording).

[3] *Six Choral Folk-Songs*, op. 36[b].

[4] *There Was a Tree*: no. 2 of *Six Choral Folk-Songs*, op. 36[b].

[5] *At the Boar's Head*: a musical interlude in one act, op. 42. During an illness, Holst was reading Shakespeare's *Henry IV* and noticed that phrases from the play fitted naturally several English folk tunes. He then decided to compose a complete opera on this basis.

146   Thaxted.

Oct 31 [1924]

Dear Will,

Thank you for your lovely dirge.[1] It is a joy to see it in print and the Trust is to be congratulated.

Thanks too for the male voice setting of the first thing Morley sang under you. I shall never forget that night. I sang 1st bass next to a chap who had been through the Mons retreat and between you, it and him the effect was overwhelming.

Please send it to Davison.[2]

I hope to hear your 2nd Byrd performance in London.[3] Is there a chance of your having a meal alone with me? Parties and crowds take it out of me horribly.

Yrs Ever,

G

[1] Whittaker's *A Lyke-Wake Dirge* for chorus and orchestra, published by Stainer & Bell Ltd. for the Carnegie United Kingdom Trust.

[2] Archibald T. Davison, Professor of Choral Music at Harvard University and conductor of the Harvard Glee Club.

[3] Whittaker conducted the Newcastle Bach Choir in a performance of Byrd's *'Great' Service* at St Margaret's church, Westminster, on 25 November.

147

Thaxted,
Dunmow.

20 November [1924]

Dear Will,

I'm very sorry but I find it impossible to come to town this weekend and so I must miss both you and Byrd.

My head has been bad for the last four days and I'm only fit for solitary walking, reading by the fire or bed. I hope to be fit again in a week but until then I must be here and alone.

The Best of Success to you.

Yrs,

Gustav

Don't trouble to answer.

148

Thaxted.

Dec 8 [1924]

Dear Will,

Thanks for letter and JSB. In your next cantata I wish you would mention the price and try and simplify the piano part in the first chorus. The editing seems admirable to me.

If TCL[1] is what it was 30 years ago I fear I congratulate you on your escape!

I was very sorry to miss your triumph in London. I gather that you and your singers scored more heavily than Byrd and I am still wondering whether that Service is the Man at his best.

Barring occasional twinges and a flabby arm I'm all right now.

Yrs Ever,

G

---

[1] Trinity College, London (now Trinity College of Music), where Holst had been unsuccessful in obtaining a composition scholarship before he went to the Royal College of Music in 1893.

149   32 Gunterstone Road,
                                                    Barons Court, W.14.

                                                    Feb 9 [1925]
Dear Will,

Thank you for both. I don't think the song is one of your best but I'll
wait until I hear it sung by the dedicatee. As far as I have read it the book
(on JSB)[1] seems to me your very best or anyhow one of them. Congratulations.

                                    Yrs,

                                    Gustav

---

[1] Whittaker's *Fugitive Notes on Certain Cantatas and the Motets of J. S. Bach*
(Oxford, 1924), a collection of articles reprinted from the *Organist and Choirmaster*.

150   32 Gunterstone Road,
                                                    Barons Court, W.14.

                                                    March 3 [1925]
Dear Will,

Thanks for the Coelestial Spheare.[1] I am sorry I cannot like it more than
I do and I fear that what has happened to many others is happening to
us. Namely, that as we develop each one's mode of expression becomes
harder for the other to grasp. Anyhow this is so on my side and my only
consolation is that I have learnt on former occasions that it need not alter
friendships.

Of course it may only mean that I am stupider than I was two years ago
—I certainly feel so!

Whatever the cause, I cannot get hold of your new work and neither does
it get hold of me. And I am very sorry.

Good luck to March 31.[2] I hope to goodness that I can be in London and
free to go that night. All is clear so far but my new opera[3] is coming out at
Manchester on April 3.

                                    Yrs Ever,

                                    Gustav

---

[1] *The Coelestial Spheare*: a poem by W. Habington, set to music by Whittaker
for chorus and orchestra.

[2] The first performance of Whittaker's *A Lyke-Wake Dirge* for chorus and
orchestra, given in the Central Hall, Westminster, by the London Bach Choir
conducted by Ralph Vaughan Williams.

[3] *At the Boar's Head*, op. 42.

151   St Paul's Girls' School,
                                                        Brook Green,
                                                        Hammersmith, W.6.

                                                        Mar. 12th, 1925

Dear Will,

I believe The Boar's Head is to be done in Swansea during Easter Week
and then at Golders Green, Hampstead, the week after that so that the
chances of your hearing it soon seem rather remote. Probably the piano
score will be available by the 25th of this month and of course you will
be one of the first to receive a copy so perhaps that would suit you. I wish
I could send you a copy of my Choral Symphony[1] for Leeds but it is
important that nobody writes about it for some time to come. Good luck
to the 4th of April![2]

                                        Yours ever,

                                               Gustav

[1] *First Choral Symphony*, op. 41.
[2] A performance of Bach's *St Matthew Passion* in Newcastle, conducted by
Whittaker.

152   The British National Opera
                                                        Company Ltd.,
                                                        Manchester.

                                                        March 27 [1925]

Dear Will,

Please accept this.[1] It will be done in Cardiff April 7 and 17 also at the
Hippodrome, Golders Green London on April 20 and 29.

We are rehearsing every day and to my great regret I find it impossible
to come back to London to hear the Dirge.[2]

It is a great disappointment for I admire the work very much.

Best of good luck.

                                        Yrs,

                                               Gustav

[1] A copy of the score of *At the Boar's Head*, op. 42.
[2] Whittaker's *A Lyke-Wake Dirge*.

153

Brook End,
Easton Park,
Dunmow.

April 14 [1925]

Dear Will,

It was good to hear and read of your success at Queen's Hall and it was a great disappointment to have to miss it. On the Monday I had wild ideas of rushing up to town just for the night but on the Tuesday I had to chuck rehearsals and go to bed with the pleasant result that I felt in fine form for the show on Friday.

I hear from Vally that you may be in London next Monday the 20th. If so will you come with me to the 'Boar's Head' and 'Gianni Schicchi' in the evening and also have a meal with me at 6 beforehand? I shall be here until the 18th after which at 32 Gunterstone Road. Will you suggest a meeting and feeding place at 6?

Yrs Ever,

Gustav

154

32 Gunterstone Road,
Barons Court, W.14.

Friday [17 April 1925]

Dear Will,

I got your letter just before leaving for home where I am now. I am inviting Mrs Fritsch[1] to come to the BH on Monday. If you both come you can catch a train at 10.15 easily which gets you in at 11.30. In any case I shall meet you at Kings X at 6.15.

Yrs in haste,

G

[1] Vally Lasker's sister Hedwig.

155

32 Gunterstone Road,
Barons Court, W.14.

9 PM April 23 [1925]

Dear Will,

This is disgusting and damnable. There are about six stations at London Bridge and two trains arrived from Dorking in two different ones within three minutes of each other and the passengers escaped from the first one on to two platforms with the result that I was a few minutes late for the second train. I wandered wildly and the things I did not say were not many neither worth saying.

I'm so sorry.

What about next week. Any luck? Wednesday would suit me better than Thursday.

Yrs Ever,

G

156

Monday [27 April 1925]

Dear Will,

I will go to Golders Green on Wed and seek a Nice Looking Feeding Shop from 6.30 to 6.50.

From 6.50 to 7.10 I will await you at the Hippodrome vestibule.

At 7.10 I will give the name and address of the above mentioned NLFS to the girl at the booking office so that she can tell you where I am if you ask her between 7.10 and 7.45.

Between 7.45 and 8 I shall swear in the vestibule until you turn up.

At 8 I shall resign myself to the worst—otherwise the BH.[1]

Yrs,

G

[1] *At the Boar's Head*, op. 42.

157

32 Gunterstone Road,
W.14.

[6 July 1925]

I arrive at Charing X at 6.30 on Wed (from Deal). Could you meet me then and have a meal? And would Mary come too?

Yrs,

G

158   St Paul's Girls' School,
                                                          Brook Green,
                                                          Hammersmith, W.6.

                                                          Nov 6 [1925]

Dear Will,

It seems wrong for you to be coming to the Jolly Talgarth[1] without a
chance of meeting. So here's love and greeting to you and Mary with many
thanks for your letter and for the beautiful performance of the H of J.
As for the audience—but I've no language left for N o T.[2]

                           Yrs Ever,
                              G

[1] Holst's nickname for Vally Lasker's house at 103 Talgarth Road, London W14.
[2] Newcastle upon Tyne.

159   St Paul's Girls' School,
                                                          Brook Green,
                                                          Hammersmith, W.6.

                                                          [25 November 1925]

  Rather!
    Not 'alf!!
      You bet!!!

                              G

160   St Paul's Girls' School,
                                                          Brook Green,
                                                          Hammersmith, W.6.

                                                          Dec. 15th, 1925

Dear Will,

Thank you for a most delightful Christmas present. I shall keep the
letter as it will always be a delight to me especially as the writer has voiced
what I am sure many others in Newcastle feel with regard to you. I wish

I could have heard your singers sing *The Urn*.[1] Perhaps I shall have that luck some day.

The best of Christmases to you.

Yours ever,

Gustav

[1] *Ode on a Grecian Urn*: third movement of the *First Choral Symphony*, op. 41.

161

Brook End,
Easton Park,
Dunmow.

Xmas Day [1925]

Dear Will,

Thanks for and congratulations on the Bach scores. They were badly needed and are well done and should be popular. Certainly I shall do my best to make them so. Your ad lib violin III is excellent. When I spoke to you about it at Leeds I was under the impression that you were having a 3d violin part dished up instead of viola and was naturally distressed.

Hope to see you in 10 days time. Shall be in London on Tuesday next.

Yrs Ever,

Gustav

162

St Paul's Girls' School,
Brook Green,
Hammersmith, W.6.

Dec 29 [1925]

Dear Will,

I am sorry I cannot put you up and cannot think how the mistake arose. I believe Vally is expecting you and anyhow she is writing. I want you and her to come to the theatre with me on Thursday the 7th. I stupidly told her that I should be free on Tuesday but forgot that I was booked that night.

Yrs,

G

163
St Paul's Girls' School,
Brook Green,
Hammersmith, W.6.

Jan. 25th, 1926

Dear Will,

Will you send the score of "Squire Dacre"[1] to Sir Henry Wood, 4, Elsworthy Road, N.W. I have ascertained that now is the time to send him scores and I am writing to tell him that I have advised you to do this. I look forward to seeing you at the Newcastle station barrier at 12.20 next Friday and also look forward to your putting me into a train that will get me to Glasgow in ample time for my lecture.[2]

Yours ever,

Gustav

[1] Whittaker's arrangement of *Noble Squire Dacre*.
[2] The fifth in his series of Cramb lectures at the University of Glasgow.

164
Glasgow.

Friday [12 February 1926]

Of course you may.

Yrs,
G

165
St Paul's Girls' School,
Brook Green,
Hammersmith, W.6.

Mar. 19th, 1926

Dear Will,

Thanks for letter. Am delighted that you had such a success. I am sorry I forgot about the printed tympany part. I have no recollection of it whatsoever. Congratulations on the Melbourne articles which interested me greatly. I fear I made a bad mistake in talking to you about the Keats

Symphony[1] as I never meant that I liked the Finale best. I think the work as a whole is the best thing I have written and, like you, I prefer the two middle movements.

Yours sincerely,

Gustav

[1] *First Choral Symphony*, op. 41.

166

St Paul's Girls' School,
Brook Green,
Hammersmith, W.6.

[17 June 1926]

Do you mind if I don't? I did so much jawing last winter[1] that I want to give it up at least for a year or two.

Yrs,

G

[1] Holst had given lectures in various places, including a series on 'England and her Music' at Liverpool University and the series of Cramb lectures at Glasgow University.

167

St Paul's Girls' School,
Brook Green,
Hammersmith, W.6.

June 28th, 1926

Dear Will,

I was very sorry to receive enclosed; doubtless you have heard from him also, but knowing our man we can be quite certain that it is only a pleasure deferred.

I was delighted to hear from Vally of your proposed holiday. When are you in London next?

Yours ever,

Gustav

St Paul's Girls' School,
Brook Green,
Hammersmith, W.6.

July 1 [1926]

I shall be coming from Dorking on Sat arriving at Waterloo about
5.30 PM. Could you meet me there? Or would you send me a card c/o
Mrs Fritsch, Danesmount, Tower Hill, Dorking by Sat morning, letting
me know where to meet you. Vally would give us a meal if you like.

Yrs,

G

169

Brook End,
Easton Park,
Dunmow.

Aug 8 [1926]

Yr cable from Rome has been forwarded and I have written to Curwens.
But I am quite bewildered as Mrs D[1] cabled to me a month ago for Savitri
score and parts. I gave the cable to Curwens and they cabled to her that the
material was being sent!

Well don't let this or anything else spoil Italy and your holiday. We
all hope and expect this latter to be the Event of the Year!

Yrs,

G

[1] Louise B. M. Dyer.

170

St Paul's Girls' School,
Brook Green,
Hammersmith, W.6.

20 September [1926]

Dear Will,

I hope
a) you've had a great time abroad

b) you're having another now even if it is a bit strenuous

c) you'll accept these

d) that we'll meet at the JT[1] or some other equally delectable place before long.

Yrs ever,

Gustav

[1] Jolly Talgarth.

171

St Paul's Girls' School,
Brook Green,
Hammersmith, W.6.

Nov 3 [1926]

I wrote to Curwens at once and they have already written to Mrs Dyer. I don't know what they have said but I don't think that there will be any bother.

I'd like to see the correspondence re my Choral Sym that you promised me but there is no hurry.

Yrs,

G

172

[Edinburgh]

[9 November 1926]

I'll write to Allen[1] re Glasgow on Monday. Give yr hostess my love. The Reid orchestra is rough but willing and I think they will do themselves justice.

Yrs,

GH

[1] Hugh P. Allen.

173

St Paul's Girls' School,
Brook Green,
Hammersmith, W.6.

Nov 16 [1926]

Dear Will,

Yr letter arrived this evening. This morning I wrote to Allen. My advice is that you write to the latter saying that I told you to. I told him no details so you can mention as much or as little as you like. It might be wise to try and see him when you come to town so ask for an appointment and ring up RCM for the answer. I know no one in authority in Glasgow but I go there to conduct on Dec 2nd and may be able to get in a word.

Let me know if there is anything else I can do. I wrote to California some time ago telling them to snap you up before it was too late.

As for AC[1] I used up all my bad language long ago. The name is just a dirty smell to me that I want to forget—and shall do when you quit.

I'd better stop!

Yrs,

G

When and where do we meet this weekend?

[1] Armstrong College.

174

SPGS

Sat [20 November 1926]

Will you
a) lunch with me on Wed
b) name the hour
c) ,, ,, place or
d) ,, where you will be just before.

Yrs,

G

175

St Paul's Girls' School,
Brook Green,
Hammersmith, W.6.

Dec 22 [1926]

Dear Will,

I send enclosed (without the writer's permission) because I think it is as nice a compliment as one could possibly have. Especially coming from a charming wife of a charming ex-professor[1] of the Leeds University.

With all Xmas greetings,

Yrs,

Gustav

I imagine that the post is not good enough for you to contemplate.

[1] Julius B. Cohen, formerly Professor of Organic Chemistry at the University of Leeds.

176

St Paul's Girls' School,
Brook Green,
Hammersmith, W.6.

Jan 24th, 1927

Dear Will,

The Cohens are coming to London early in February and I hope to have a long talk. I do not feel I know them well enough to discuss things by post. Also I do not understand University matters. Could you write a list of points for me to put to them? Also, am I to refer to the possibility of your leaving Armstrong?

Yours sincerely,

Gustav

177

St Paul's Girls' School,
Brook Green,
Hammersmith, W.6.

Jan 26 [1927]

Could meet you anywhere on Sat after 7.15 if I hear from you that morning. I suggest Kings X station if you are leaving early.

If I don't hear from you I shall conclude it is no go.

Yrs,

G

178

St Paul's Girls' School,
Brook Green,
Hammersmith, W.6.

Feb. 7th, 1927

Dear Will,

I saw the Cohens last week and we agreed that I should write informally to him re the professorship. I send you a duplicate of the letter[1] I am sending him. I have pitched it rather strong, but this is an occasion for doing so. The only things I can tell you about the post are that it is not likely to be more than six hundred a year and that the authorities would allow their professor to do plenty of outside work. I understand that the present music lecturer has no chance.

Yours ever,

Gustav

[1] See Appendix 2.

179

St Paul's Girls' School,
Brook Green,
Hammersmith, W.6.

Feb. 14th, 1927

Dear Will,

I do not understand University matters and therefore I will not move without your consent. Would you like me to tell Cohen that I fear it is no use Leeds approaching you unless they are prepared to offer £800 a year? Let me know if there is any other thing I can do as regards Leeds or Glasgow. I expect that the latter would mean twice as much money and three times as much work as the former. Congratulations on Frankfurt, but have you to bring your own choir? When are you in town next?

Yours ever,

Gustav

180   St Paul's Girls' School,
                          Brook Green,
                          Hammersmith, W.6.

Feb 24 [1927]

Dear Will,

Walford Davies told me yesterday that he is going to Windsor.[1] This was not in confidence but it is not to be passed on. We only met in a hurry and in public—I put in a word for you. Leeds finds it difficult to raise enough money.

I wish I could do something really helpful.

Yrs,

G

[1] Davies commenced his duties as organist of St George's Chapel in September 1927.

181   [Great Driffield,
                          Yorkshire]

[15 April 1927]

When you go to Beverley Minster tell the verger that you are a musician and he'll show you the 14th century town band. When you come to the pipe and tabor ask him (the verger not the piper) for his story of Dancing Ducks. I am on a walking tour (I mean a '"Walking"' (?!!) one).

Yrs,

Gustav

182

St Paul's Girls' School,
Brook Green,
Hammersmith, W.6.

May 9th, 1927

Dear Will,

You are probably much too busy to write, but could you send me a card telling me the address of Mrs Dyer when she arrives in England. Last time she was here I was feeling very seedy and would like to make amends and give her a really good time.

The best of luck to you in Frankfurt and elsewhere. I hear that you are looking thoroughly overworked already, which is a bad start for a term, but I have also heard that you are going to have a first-rate holiday abroad.

Yours ever,

Gustav

183

[Hammersmith,
London, W.6.]

[7 September 1927]

No (They were from 5 to 6 I think). Good luck to you and them with love to AKH.[1] When do we meet?

Yrs,

G

P.S. Just a little warning—if you ever ask me to lecture again I shall probably accept! I've given up trying to reform!

[1] Arthur K. Holland, author and music critic of the *Liverpool Daily Post*.

184

St Paul's Girls' School,
Brook Green,
Hammersmith, W.6.

Oct 28 [1927]

Dear Will,

Thanks for the new partsong. It is always good to get your things and this one ranks high. In fact I am inclined to put it only below the very best such as 'Blow the wind' and 'Bonny'.

I'm glad you've met the Wilkinsons and hope you liked them as much as they liked you.

I hear a rumour that the Liverpool professorship is in the 'offing' but don't know what it will be like or worth and perhaps you are not considering its possibilities.

I'm hoping to have a month at Xmas in Vienna and Prague!

Yrs Ever,

Gustav

185

St Paul's Girls' School,
Brook Green,
Hammersmith, W.6.

Dec 9 [1927]

Greetings to you and your hosts.[1]

Gustav

[1] Addressed to Whittaker c/o the Sandon Club, Liberty Buildings, Liverpool.

186

St Paul's Girls' School,
Brook Green,
Hammersmith, W.6.

Jan 26 [1928]

Dear Will,

Thank you for your delightful present. Having read her 'Wandering Scholars'[1] I was delighted to have another book of Waddell. And the 'Be not afraid' picture is a real joy.

I would have written before but have been away in Vienna and Prague—a wonderful time.

I've never stayed in a Vienna hotel.

I believe the 'Meisol und Schadn' Neuer Mark 2 is good and not too dear.

If private rooms are wanted I stayed at

Herr Schweinburg
Ungargasse 4
Wien III

103

and had a lovely time. The hot bath there is a myth but the kindliness and comfort and sense of freedom were facts.

Other private rooms where a girl and her parents stayed are

Frau Hollman

Luftbandgasse 5 VI

Frau Speyer

Argentinerstrasse 7 I

but I don't know them personally.

Please accept copy of my 'latest' that follows this. When do we meet?

Yrs,

G

[1] Clifford Bax's libretto for Holst's one-act chamber opera *The Tale of the Wandering Scholar*, op. 50, was based on an incident in this book by Helen Waddell.

187

St Paul's Girls' School,
Brook Green,
Hammersmith, W.6.

[8 February 1928]

I'm afraid I shall be out of town on the 18th. When's the next chance? And shall you be staying at 103[1] because if you are I shall invite myself there also!

Yrs,

G

[1] Vally Lasker's house at 103 Talgarth Road, London W14.

188

Brook End,
Dunmow,
Essex.

April 18 [1928]

Dear Will,

Thanks for the songs which have been forwarded to me here at home. I feel that I cannot judge them properly as I am only just getting over some sort of internal chill that spoilt my temper and other things last week in

Chester. Previously I had had a glorious walk in Shropshire. I am now playing the professional invalid with great success and enjoying it thoroughly. But my brain is not active and I am putting off the knowing of your new works until next week.

I have conducted the 'GG'[1] three times, only one of which was with action and am quite convinced that it makes a good concert piece.

Of course Jane's[2] story must be in the program. It <u>might</u> be better to make a slight cut. But a better plan is to have a separate choir of children to sing the 'Mummers'.

As you say, We Must Meet. Vally's flat is obviously the place and the time is your next London visit. Vally shall have the pleasure of putting us both up.

Yrs Ever,
G

[1] *The Golden Goose*: choral ballet, op. 45 no. 1.
[2] Jane M. Joseph, who wrote the words for the work, adapting a story by Grimm.

189

St Paul's Girls' School,
Brook Green,
Hammersmith, W.6.

May 8 [1928]

Dear Will,

VL is not moving. I will go to 103 on Wed night and endeavour to get your breakfast on Thursday morning. I am studying the different methods of doing this. The best one I have found so far is to get out of bed at 7 or 8 or whenever you ring, then a) let you in, b) light the gas fire, c) show you where things are, d) let you loose to do your damdest, e) go back to bed and have a good nap until you tell me that breakfast is ready

<u>unless</u>

f) you would like to bring me mine on a tray to my bedside.

Yrs,
G

P.S. That's not <u>my</u> idea of hospitality! V[1] —Prig!![2]

[1] In Vally Lasker's hand.
[2] In Holst's hand.

190

St Paul's Girls' School,
Brook Green,
Hammersmith, W.6.

Oct. 9th 1928

Dear Will,

Welcome home! I hope you have had a really good time. Probably you are too busy to write now, but would you get Potts[1] to let me know if December 1st is definitely settled for my lecture? I had hoped that he could alter it so that I could hear your performance of The Golden Goose.

With regard to the illustrations for my lecture, please do not do them all if they are too many. The important ones are: Who shall have my lady fair; Lay a garland; and In Dulci Jubilo.[2]

Shall you be coming to London? If so, give me plenty of warning as I do not want to miss seeing you. If you are not, we must wait till December 1st, when I hope we shall have a good time together.

Yours ever,

Gustav

[1] Ernest J. Potts, bass singer, of Newcastle upon Tyne.
[2] Works by Robert Pearsall.

191

[Hammersmith,
London, W.6.]

Oct 12 [1928]

Thanks for letter.

I shall hope to see you each time you are in town even if only for a few minutes.

Shall I come up North on Friday Nov 30 and have a rehearsal that night?

I cannot stay over Monday so I suggest I travel back by the night train after the lecture and get to London early on the Sunday in the chance of seeing you.

Yrs,

G

192

St Paul's Girls' School,
Brook Green,
Hammersmith, W.6.

Oct 31 [1928]

Dear Will,

For my Pearsall lecture I suggest

Song of the Franc-Companies	Yearbook Press
Who shall have	,,
In dulci	,,
Take heed	Novello
Lay a garland	,,

If you agree would you return those copies I sent Potts?
It was good to see you again.

Yrs,

G

Nov 1

Yr card just arrived.

If list on other side gives any bother let me know. I would prefer the Year Book version of In dulci (which can be wangled in places) but if it is too much of a bother we will do the Novello edition.

This list will be quite enough.

193

St Paul's Girls' School,
Brook Green,
Hammersmith, W.6.

Nov 26 [1928]

If it is not too late I would like to include Pearsall's 'Blessed Word of God' and in order to save time I am asking S and B[1] to send a dozen copies to you.

If it is too late please don't let anyone go to any bother about it—we will simply do without it. But it is quite easy.

Yrs,

G

[1] Stainer & Bell Ltd.

194
St Paul's Girls' School,
Brook Green,
Hammersmith, W.6.

[28 November 1928]

This is very good of you and I am most sorry to have given you so much bother.

Yrs,

G

When we meet on Sunday morning I want a few hints about that wonderful walk along the Roman Wall for a friend.

195   SPGS

April 19 [1929]

Dear Will,

I am sorry you are not leaving Newcastle and I am very sorry that you are sorry.

But I am not sorry at all that you are probably not going to that Philadelphia post. I heard something about it from a very good man—Davison[1] of Harvard—and I am not sure (to put it mildly) that you'd like it. As I understand it, the post is chiefly an organising one. Need I write more?

I may hear more details and I may think the post a good one but I don't at present.

I'd like to think of you planted as general musical boss at a nice USA university. And I'd like you to get Glasgow. In fact there are lots of places outside Newcastle where I have wished you to be during the last 15 years. But the Curtis Institute is not one of them—yet.

I've had The perfect walk. Four days in Dorset and Wilts; 2 miles per hour with 30 min rest for each 60 walking when fresh and the reverse when not; only 4 miles main road to 50 on grass and about 12 lanes and woodland paths: no collar, lots of cider and cheese and only one blister!

I hope your Easter has been equally successful.

Yrs Ever,

G

[1] Archibald T. Davison.

196

St Paul's Girls' School,
Brook Green,
Hammersmith, W.6.

June 2 [1929]

Dear Will,

I could write to HPA,[1] Walford Davies or Bissett. But I could not add anything to what I have already told them and if I were one of them I should resent being bothered. But I fancy I am alone in feeling that way about it. If you think it would help if I wrote to any one or all send me a pc—I don't know Bissett's address.

It was good to hear of your performance of the Tallis.[2] I would I could have heard it.

Yrs Ever,

Gustav

I am asking for a ticket for Thursday night in case you can come.

[1] Hugh P. Allen.
[2] A performance of Tallis' 40-part motet *Spem in Alium*, given in Newcastle Cathedral by the Newcastle Bach Choir conducted by Whittaker.

197

St Paul's Girls' School,
Brook Green,
Hammersmith, W.6.

Sep 15 [1929]

Dear Will,

I expect you are home by now so I send you my congratulations[1] without further delay. I also congratulate Glasgow!

It is good to know that I shall dine with you in Oxford next Sunday night. Unless I hear to the contrary I shall conclude that you do not want me to tell Balfour[2] and Fred[3] about Glasgow. All the same I should like to—they are both discreet about such things.

Yrs Ever,

G

Hope your holiday has been as good as mine.

[1] On Whittaker's appointment as Gardiner Professor of Music at the University of Glasgow.
[2] Henry Balfour Gardiner.
[3] Fred Wilkinson.

198
St Paul's Girls' School,
Brook Green,
Hammersmith, W.6.

Dec 19 [1929]

Dear Will,

I send you this[1] with my warmest greetings. You will find most of the tales soothing in the midst of all your labours and worries while settling down. When once you are fairly fixed in Glasgow I believe that you will be recognised and honoured by people whose regard will mean much. I know of no place where I would prefer you to be and I know no man whom I want to see in your post as much as I want to see you.

So it's a case of congratulations all round—to Glasgow as well as to you.

Yrs Ever,

Gustav

P.S. Don't bother to write.
P.P.S. Begin with the 'Demon Pope'.
PPPS. Glasgow has only one drawback as compared to Newcastle—it's further from the Jolly Talgarth!
PPPPS Therefore you will need to be constantly making special efforts to keep in touch with this part of the world.
PPPPPS So Make Them!

[1] Probably Richard Garnett's *The Twilight of the Gods, and other tales* (John Lane, reprinted 1927), which includes the story 'The Demon Pope'.

199
St Paul's Girls' School,
Brook Green,
Hammersmith, W.6.

Jan 6 [1930]

Dear Will,

I send this to welcome you in your Vita Nuova—what I believe will prove to be your 'spiritual home'—the place where you will be respected, honoured and loved for what you are and for what you do.

It is good to know that for the first time in your life you will have leisure. Being something new it will be all the more valuable and valued and will therefore bring a fresh value to your work.

Yrs ever,

Gustav

200
St Paul's Girls' School,
Brook Green,
Hammersmith, W.6.

Dec 30 [1930]

Dear Will,

I suppose you saw last Sat's Times.[1] It was a real feather in your cap. And today I've had a long rambling letter from Paggi which is another.

So the best thing I can wish you for 1931 is that you carry on as you have begun especially as regards being recognised and respected.

Do you know that I no longer want to cuss Newcastle—I'm only sorry for it!

Jane Joseph arranged and translated this Bach aria for me two years ago and we never did it. Would you care to publish it in your OUP series?[2]

There is no hurry for a reply.

Yrs Ever,

Gustav

[1] A review of Whittaker's arrangement for string orchestra of Purcell's *Chaconne in G minor*, recently published in the Oxford Orchestral Series, appeared in *The Times* for 27 December 1930.

[2] Whittaker was General Editor of the Oxford Choral Songs series, published by the Oxford University Press.

201
St Paul's Girls' School,
Brook Green,
Hammersmith, W.6.

Jan 11 [1931]

Dear Will,

Thank you for the score which is a delight. I can't think how I missed your edition of the JSB aria. I'll make up for lost time!

I'm thinking of having four days' holiday in Durham at the end of this week and for the first time in my life I wish you were in Newcastle so that we could meet!

Yrs Ever,

Gustav

202
St Paul's Girls' School,
Brook Green,
Hammersmith, W.6.

Feb 6 [1931]

Dear Will,

Of course Glasgow hasn't had as much BM[1] as Newcastle because it hasn't had so much WGW: You wait and see!—Or you wait and we'll see. I didn't realise it was a str concerto class. And I didn't realise that Glasgow musicians were poor. Tut tut! Also Good Luck.

Yrs,

G

[1] Probably British music, deriving from the initials of the British Music Society.

203
St Paul's Girls' School,
Brook Green,
Hammersmith, W.6.

March 16 [1931]

Dear Will,

A Mr Basil Hogarth of Glasgow has written to me about various matters; amongst other things, he wants to do Savitri and is unable to get all the necessary players. I told him that I felt sure you would help him if you could and also told him to write to you mentioning my name. I hope I've done right and that he won't be a worry. Of course you may know him quite well and he may be a good friend of yours in which case all is well.

Yrs Ever,

G

If all is well, celebrate the event by not bothering to answer this.

204

St Paul's Girls' School,
Brook Green,
Hammersmith, W.6.

May 11th, 1931

Dear Will,

Many thanks. It is wonderful to realise how you manage to make your influence felt in the USA while working fourteen hours a day in Glasgow. Please continue! The only alteration in your life I would like to suggest is that you arrange to have a meeting in London so that we can stay at "The Jolly Talgarth" again. Remember, I know where the eggs are now!

Yours ever,

Gustav

I send you my latest.[1] It is to be produced at Gloucester next September.

[1] *A Choral Fantasia* for soprano solo (or semi-chorus), chorus, organ, strings, brass and percussion, op. 51.

205

St Paul's Girls' School,
Brook Green,
Hammersmith, W.6.

July 21 [1931]

I am asking Curwen's to send you two scores of Jane's[1] which have been published. Mrs Joseph will be so glad to feel that you have them.

Yrs,

G

[1] Jane M. Joseph, who died in 1929. An appreciation of her work by Holst was published in the *Monthly Musical Record* for April 1931.

206

St Paul's Girls' School,
Brook Green,
Hammersmith, W.6.

Oct 1 [1931]

Please may I have a Talgarthian breakfast with you on Sat? And I am
hoping that a) there will be a ticket for the matinee of the Fledermaus at
Covent Garden: and b) that you will use it.

Yrs Ever,

G

(don't bother to reply)

207

St Paul's Girls' School,
Brook Green,
Hammersmith, W.6.

Nov. 2nd, 1931

Dear Will,

I am sorry I cannot cook eggs for you and have a good talk. With regard
to the evening of November 12th, we are going to a recital of Welsh
Folksongs at Cecil Sharp House, given by Mrs Herbert Jones.[1] Would you
care to meet at seven at Fleming's (near Oxford Circus). Vally is bringing
Mrs Gunn and I am bringing Diana Awdry, Mrs Jones (the singer), and
my old friend, Miss Rodwell Jones.[2] If this suits you, I will order a table.
Shall we both be hosts? If you do not go away that night, I hope we can
meet the next morning.

Yours ever,

G

[1] It was the singing of Dora Herbert Jones that gave Holst the idea of making
his arrangements of the *Twelve Welsh Folk-Songs* for unaccompanied mixed voices.
[2] Mabel Rodwell Jones.

208   Harvard University,
                                                    Division of Music,
                                                    Cambridge,
                                                    Massachusetts.
                                                    Feb 14 [1932]

Dear Will,

I send you my deepest sympathy. It was a privilege and a joy to know your mother even as little as I did. I can only guess what she must have been to you. Please give my sympathy to your father who, I hope, is well.

I had a wild time when I arrived[1]—three entire symphony concerts to conduct as well as four rehearsals. Now I'm settling down to teach composition here. They have given me delightful rooms and I find that I can get a fair amount of writing done. What a good fellow is Duncan MacKenzie. He was most helpful when I was in New York.

You will be too busy to write but I hope to get news of you from Vally and others. I suppose you still breakfast at 103—I hope I may cook you eggs there in July if not before.

Yrs Ever,

Gustav

[1] Holst was treated as a celebrity on this visit to the USA. He was interviewed by various journalists, and the resulting articles included 'Holst in America: an interview with one of the first contemporary composers to conduct his own works for recording' by R. D. Darrell, published in the February issue of *Phonograph Monthly Review*, and 'Gustav Holst, on America visit approves our ways' by Quaintance Eaton, published in *Musical America* for 10 February 1932.

209   Harvard University,
                                                    Division of Music,
                                                    Cambridge,
                                                    Massachusetts.

                                                    March 17, 1932

Dear Will,

Thank you for your three letters. I am most grateful to you for your wonderful performance of my "Fantasia"[1] and wish I could have been there to hear it. Please give my thanks to your singers and players.

I am deeply sorry to hear about your father.

I hope to be back on July 1. Try and fix up a London visit with a J.T. breakfast.

Yours ever,

Gustav

[1] *A Choral Fantasia*, op. 51.

210

Harvard University,
Division of Music,
Cambridge,
Massachusetts.

May 12 [1932]

Dear Will,

If you've reached the stage of not daring to write to me you must indeed be in need of a holiday p.d.q! I shall probably be back about June 8. Any chance of seeing you at the JT or elsewhere en route for Eisenach? I dare not promise anything as I hope my brother[1] will come back with me for a short holiday and I want to be with him in June—we are going to stroll over the Cotswolds together for the first time for over 40 years! But I'd do my best to meet you.

Re lecture. I can't promise anything until after my return but of course I'd like to come if the date suited.

I've only one new lecture and that's on Haydn[2] and it's too short. (I gave it at Washington and the Roth quartet played divinely.) Also it will be probably out of date by the autumn! Between ourselves I wish I could either a) abandon lecturing or b) do it better.

People keep on tempting me and in many matters it is sound policy to fall if sufficiently tempted. But does this apply to gas escapes? Anyhow get the ISM[3] to write to me at SPGS at end of June. I always try to get £10··10 and 1st class fare and sometimes I succeed—quite often in fact. But of course I'm open to hints from you. And that weekend with you and JSB is most alluring.

Have a Thundering Good Time abroad.

Yrs Ever,

Gustav

[1] Emil von Holst (Ernest Cossart, the actor).
[2] This lecture was published in *Heirs and Rebels* (Oxford, 1959).
[3] Incorporated Society of Musicians.

211

St Paul's Girls' School,
Brook Green,
London W6.

July 19 [1932]

Dear Will,

Thanks for a nice long letter. It is good to know that you are having such a good time although I don't approve of 35 letters per day when on holiday and almost feel inclined to apologise for this one!

Also I doubt whether wallowing in church cantatas by JSB's uncles and cousins is really a change of occupation.

As for me I was in hospital at the end of March with a duodenal ulcer. They say that there is good in all things. Anyhow they said so when I was a boy. If it is true then I should be grateful to that ulcer because it taught me the real meaning of the phrase 'a bloody nuisance'.

It upset some of my plans—I escaped a Conference of Music Supervisors in Cincinnati and was unable to conduct 'Hammersmith'[1] at Washington and had to abandon a trip through Canada from Vancouver Island to Quebec. And after leaving hospital I developed a severe attack of home sickness.

I'm all right now except that my walking is even more middle-aged than before and I've got to keep off alcohol which I don't mind and fresh fruit which I do.

Except for short walks—I mean 'walks' (?)—I shall be in London until the Worcester Festival and shall be alone in Talgarth Rd except when my wife joins me from time to time.

So let us foregather soon and long.

While in Harvard I began writing some male voice things.[2] Since my return I've been indulging in canons.[3] One of them is for two choirs and three keys. However the attack is nearly over and I don't think I shall repeat the offense.

Yrs Ever,

Gustav

P.S. Don't come back between Aug 14 and 20 because I shall be in the Cotswolds part of that week with a New York actress with whom I fell in love. She will be accompanied by her aunt and cousin but they are old pals of mine and they won't get in the way seriously so I am looking forward to a good time.

[1] *Hammersmith*: prelude and scherzo for military band, op. 52 (also arranged for orchestra). This was to have been the first performance of the original military band version of the work, which remained unplayed until 1954 when Robert Cantrick conducted its first performance in Pittsburgh, Pennsylvania.

[2] *Six Choruses* for male voices, strings, organ or piano.

[3] *Eight Canons* for equal voices.

212

St Paul's Girls' School,
Brook Green,
Hammersmith, W.6.

Sep 25 [1932]

Dear Will,

I see your point re the canon. But I do like both the singers and listeners to feel the two keys quite distinctly and I think that making the former do so helps the effect to the latter. Recently I have written some three-keyed canons and I hope that if they are published in both notations[1] this distinctness will be maintained. It is something quite apart from the hits and squashes of conventional 'modern' harmony.

And I felt secretly flattered when an excellent musician complained that my two-key writing won't do because it has no 'wrong notes' in it.

Yrs Ever,

Gustav

[1] i.e. ordinary notation and tonic sol-fa.

213

St Paul's Girls' School,
Brook Green,
Hammersmith, W.6.

[10 October 1932]

I've invited myself to the JT next Thursday and shan't stop away unless you tell me to sternly.

Yrs,

G

214

St Paul's Girls' School,
Brook Green,
Hammersmith, W.6.

Oct. 17th, 1932

Dear Will,

It was nice to see you last week but I do not think I will come next time because I find it impossible to sit up at night. Although I am quite well the doctor tells me that I have got to go easy because my blood is not up to the mark either in quantity or quality as a result of my trouble in America. This should all come to an end, I hope, next Easter, but until then I must live as quietly as possible. If you are ever in London in the daytime let me know. Otherwise I shall hope to hear news of you from Vally and Mary. The worst of this business is that I cannot write. When I settle down to compose I usually fall asleep. However, it is only temporary.

Yours ever,

Gustav

215　　　　　　　　　　　　　　　　　St Paul's Girls' School,
　　　　　　　　　　　　　　　　　　　Brook Green,
　　　　　　　　　　　　　　　　　　　Hammersmith, W.6.

Nov 28 [1932]

Dear Will,

Vally is distressed (mildly) that her sofa is going phut so some of us are signing a comic Xmas letter[1] begging to be allowed to subscribe for the necessary surgical operation.

As I know you'd like to be 'in' this the document will be sent you for signature in a fortnight or so.

Yrs Ever,

G

[1] See also next letter.

216　　　　　　　　　　　　　　　　　St Paul's Girls' School,
　　　　　　　　　　　　　　　　　　　Brook Green,
　　　　　　　　　　　　　　　　　　　Hammersmith, W.6.

Dec 10 [1932]

Dear Will,

Please sign this[1] in an unexpected place and don't write too small.

Has Miss Lawton slept at the JT? And Mary? If so make them sign also. Let me have it back as soon as possible.

Yrs in haste,

G

[1] See Plate 5 and Appendix 3.

217
as from SPGS,
Brook Green.

Dec 26 [1932]

Dear Will,

Thanks for the program. We had another Purcell suite[1] ready years ago but I did not send it to Novello's because you and the others do editing work so much better than I.

I started doing those suites years ago for St Paul's when we first had wood-wind so that we could turn on music in which it did not matter whether the wind played or not. Then, for some reason which I have forgotten, I published them. We must talk over the matter now that you will be in London more. (That's a good article of yours in the Dec Mus Times.[2])

Will you be seeing Mr van Raalte?[3] If so will you give him my warmest thanks for his performance of 'Egdon Heath'. (Perhaps I should really thank you. Or perhaps it's a case of fifty-fifty.) It was not the result of that lunch with Hardy as the program stated but the result of years of knowing him, his books, and, above all, the heath. It was the first serious work I wrote after my accident ten years ago and it means much to me.

If Mr van Raalte is ever in London after the first weeks of Jan I hope he will give me the pleasure of dining with me.

We've had a week's sunshine in Essex and I had a lovely though distinctly middle-aged walk here. I hope to walk back another way into town and then come out again before term begins.

Are you getting a good holiday?

Yrs Ever,

Gustav

---

[1] *The Old Bachelor*: incidental music for strings by Henry Purcell, edited by Holst with additional wind and drum parts ad lib. The surviving manuscript score of this arrangement shows only the stringed instruments.

[2] 'The Business of a Music Editor' by Whittaker, published in the *Musical Times* for December 1932.

[3] Albert van Raalte, a Dutch conductor who gave concerts in Glasgow.

218

Great Easton,
Dunmow,
Essex.

Jan 7 [1933]

Dear Will,

I don't know what you'll think of me and all this but you'd better have [it] and then, if it won't do, you can forget it all the sooner. I don't quite know what to think of it myself but I fancy that I shall like 'David's Lament' and 'Truth of all Truth'.[1] Thanks for letter. We must have a good talk over Purcell arrangements when we meet. And we must meet soon.

So you're writing a brass band piece—Splendid! I wish you could come to Carlisle on Feb 12 and meet that Nice band master. I fear I shall not be able to call in on you in Glasgow this time.

But there's always the JT!

Yrs,

G

[1] Nos. 4 & 6 of *Eight Canons* for equal voices.

219

St Paul's Girls' School,
Brook Green,
Hammersmith, W.6.

March 16 [1933]

Dear Will,

I've put the matter to Curwen[1] who will write to you. He is always helpful when possible. You've promised not to do Savitri for some time so I hope I may be able to come up for it.

Just now I'm in bed for three weeks on a milk diet in order to get rid of the last vestige of that ulcer. I'm at Ealing but all letters are forwarded so I won't bother you with another address.

Yrs ever,

G

[1] John Curwen, of J. Curwen & Sons Ltd.

220

St Paul's Girls' School,
Brook Green,
Hammersmith, W.6.

July 26 [1933]

Dear Will,

It is good to be able to gloat over your full score. It is good to recall the joy you gave me when you first showed it to me. And it is good to realise how much your fame has grown and your worth recognised since then. For all which, my best thanks.

Yrs,

Gustav

221

St Paul's Girls' School,
Brook Green,
Hammersmith, W.6.

Oct 25 [1933]

Dear Will,

Dr Archibald Davison conductor of the Harvard Glee Club and his wife are over here and are coming to Glasgow at the end of next week and he is most anxious to meet you so I have told him to write to you at once in order to fix a meeting.

I expect you know of him and his work. He has had the Glee Club for 25 years and has transformed it from a social-function-free-and-easy-bright-and-brotherly-singsong affair into a first rate m v choir.

They were most kind to me last year and I want them to have a first rate time now. And therefore I send them to you!

Yrs Ever,

Gustav

222

St Paul's Girls' School,
Brook Green,
Hammersmith, W.6.

Dec 7 [1933]

Dear Will,

As Vally has been doing even more work for me than usual lately I have asked her whether I may answer yr letter for her.

She does not get back from Overstone until midday on Thursday. I have asked her whether I may go to 103 on Wed night and prepare a hot bath, coffee and eggs for you by 8.30 AM Thursday. She says I may. Do you?

On Friday evening I'm having a very rough try through of some of my latest things from 7.30 to 9.30. Could you stop for it? I'd like you to for my sake but not for yours. It will certainly be a 'try' but I'm doubtful about the through!

Did you do this work of Jane's?[1] If so do you remember the scoring well enough to help me rescore it? Score and parts are hopelessly lost.

It will be splendid if we can meet on Thursday.

Yrs Ever,

Gustav

[1] Jane M. Joseph.

223

St Paul's Girls' School,
Brook Green,
Hammersmith, W.6.

[early 1934]

At last I have learnt some real value in the ISM.[1] I am most grateful to it for giving me more WGW in 1933.

Yrs,

G

[1] Whittaker had been elected President of the Incorporated Society of Musicians for 1934.

224

Beaufort House,
Ealing W5.

Saturday [Spring 1934]

Dear Will,

You are the Perfect Nurse and your letter was just what I needed, especially the parts about GFH, JSB, WGW and DFT[1]—although I am not convinced that a world of Toveys would be queerer than the world as it is. In fact I don't think any world could be!

But your remarks on being a conductor are sadly out of date. In Victorian days I heard a second cornet remark 'I'm thinking of giving up music and becoming a musical director', but today the conductor is the most highly honoured of musicians and one of the most highly skilled. I feel this so strongly that I'm thinking of giving up all ideas of stickwagging in the future and asking people to engage Imogen instead. (By the way it was my missus Isobel who wrote to you not Imogen but that doesn't matter.)

To return to conducting, everyone is agreed that the highest and most difficult form of the art is operatic conducting. And when it comes to conducting Handel's operas! Well, 'there ain't no blooming words for it guv'nor' as the Cockney said when his 2nd tyre burst. At first sight it is a little puzzling to find you bracketing conducting and committees together. But I see now that my first theory was right. Wallowing in committees helps you to conduct just as wallowing in whiskey helps other artists to sing or play. There is much to be said for both but I don't approve of either. And the simplest way of breaking yourself of this bad habit is to get a Large Braw Scot with a Voice to deputise at committees for you. Explain what you want done and then tell him to go on talking until the others do it. And there you are! (Strictly speaking you are not but you know what I mean.)

Then you will have ample time to be the Perfect Nurse and sit on the JT sofa and talk to me about GFH, JSB, WGW and other nice people.

Yrs Ever,

Gustav

[1] George Frederick Handel, Johann Sebastian Bach, William Gillies Whittaker and Donald Francis Tovey.

APPENDIX 1

Letters from Holst and his pupils to W. G. Whittaker

See plate section between pages 126 and 127

(a) Letter sent to Whittaker after his visit to London in January 1918.
(b) Message of greeting (undated).

APPENDIX 2

Letter from Holst to Professor J. B. Cohen

Feb. 7th, 1927

Dear Dr Cohen,

I hear that there is a possibility of a Chair of Music being founded at Leeds University. If this is so, it might interest you to know that I believe that it might be possible to secure Dr W. G. Whittaker of Newcastle for the professorship. This is only my own opinion, but he is such a first-rate man that I cannot resist the temptation of writing to you in case it were possible to secure his services. As far as I can see there is no-one else available to equal him, both as a brilliant musician and experienced and inspiring teacher. I am sure you will agree with me that it is worth while making enquiries and that is why I write this letter to you.

I hope to have another chance of seeing you both when you are in London.

Yours sincerely,

(*unsigned carbon copy*)

APPENDIX 3

Letter sent to subscribers for the repairs to Vally Lasker's sofa

St Paul's Girls' School,
Brook Green, W.6.

March 1933

Dear Sir or Madam,

We have much pleasure in informing you that the Talgarthian Sofa has returned from the hospital well and strong and younger than ever. Your share of the cost is 2/1½, which please send to either of us when convenient.

We trust that you will excuse the delay which has been caused by the difficulty in procuring a suitable spring frock for the convalescent.

Yours faithfully,

Amy Kemp
Gustav Holst

APPENDIX 4

Letters from Whittaker to Holst

(a)
4 Granville Road,
Jesmond,
Newcastle-on-Tyne.

19/12/12

Dear Mr von Holst,

How thoughtful of you to send me your letter of good wishes, which arrived to cheer me on the morning of the concert, and which I read out to the choir before we began.

The enclosed critique gives a pretty good idea of the way the "Hymns"[1] went and the difficulties we worked against. The writer should have added that the new members were not only unaccustomed to singing "ultra-modern works", but that their former conductor had never troubled himself about such mere details as accuracy, expression, or pronunciation. It meant beginning all over again, but they have worked willingly and well, and I really think that we gave a creditable performance of your works. The first two went without a single hitch, the second being particularly impressive. In the last the altos converted one of your 7/4 bars into 6/4 (I don't blame them), and there was a little wandering round for a couple of bars, when the basses came in with confident vigour and shook everybody straight. We flattened slightly at two places. I can honestly say that with the exception of these flaws, the choir really gave an excellent account of the Funeral Hymn. Of course, those members of the audience who think Handel the final word in art were greatly puzzled by your works, but all the enlightened souls were very much impressed, and expressed, in no hesitant terms, their admiration of the originality and beauty of your compositions.

Permit me on behalf of the choir, and particularly on my own behalf, to utter an earnest "thanks" to you for writing such a splendid group of

126

PLATE 6   APPENDIX I (a)

Morley College
Waterloo Road
London, S.E. 1.
January 1918.

Dear Mr. Whittaker,

We, the undersigned Music Students of Morley College, wish to put on record the thanks which many of us have already expressed to you verbally. We want to say with how much satisfaction we look back upon the crowded activities of the week-end when you visited us. To the Choir the performance of your works under your own conductorship was a double pleasure, while to the Orchestra and Harmony Students the experience was no less one of sheer delight.

The lecture which was the primary object of your visit fulfilled our best expectations. Those of us who already knew something of Mr von Holst's music felt that we had been enabled the better to understand the relation between the different phases of his creative work, while those to whom it was unfamiliar received an introduction which made them desirous of knowing and appreciating it more fully.

It may be said that whereas before your visit many of us knew you only through your works, and Mr. von Holst only (or mainly) through his personality, your coming to Morley has gone a long way to fill up what was lacking in our knowledge on each side. We have thus to thank you for what is a double gain to us.

We would ask you to accept our cordial good wishes for the continued success of your

labours in the good cause of English music in the
North, and would also like you to convey our
fraternal greetings to your own students at
Armstrong College, whom since your visit we
regard as friends of our own.

      Believe us to be sincerely and gratefully
yours:—

[Two columns of signatures]

Wilfred Shalmas.

Vall ...

George R Nutting

J Clutterill

E. L Vine

N Coop.

J. Elvin Parker

Alice Lastrer.

J. Colven.

M. Middleton.

a. Furnival

E H Board

L E Jwinselton

Brul

M. Willshen.

G J Dyson

H. Poole

Lau Williams

Howe

G R Williams

Jas. Robertson.

Maud Smith

Margaret C Brown.

a. H. Keighley

I Hayward

More E. E. Nicholson

M. Jones.

R. C Vec S.

M. A. Ritchie

C. B. Cox.

Isold von Holst.

A. Lansdell

Chas. Fitch

Dot Pavey

M Watter

R Murphy

J Johnson

A Delafons

D. Bird.

Ea Squire

W Morris

H Beard

N Hayes.

C. A. Peebles.

Geo G. Lewis

C Morant

E. White.

Mary Clarke

I Hammersley

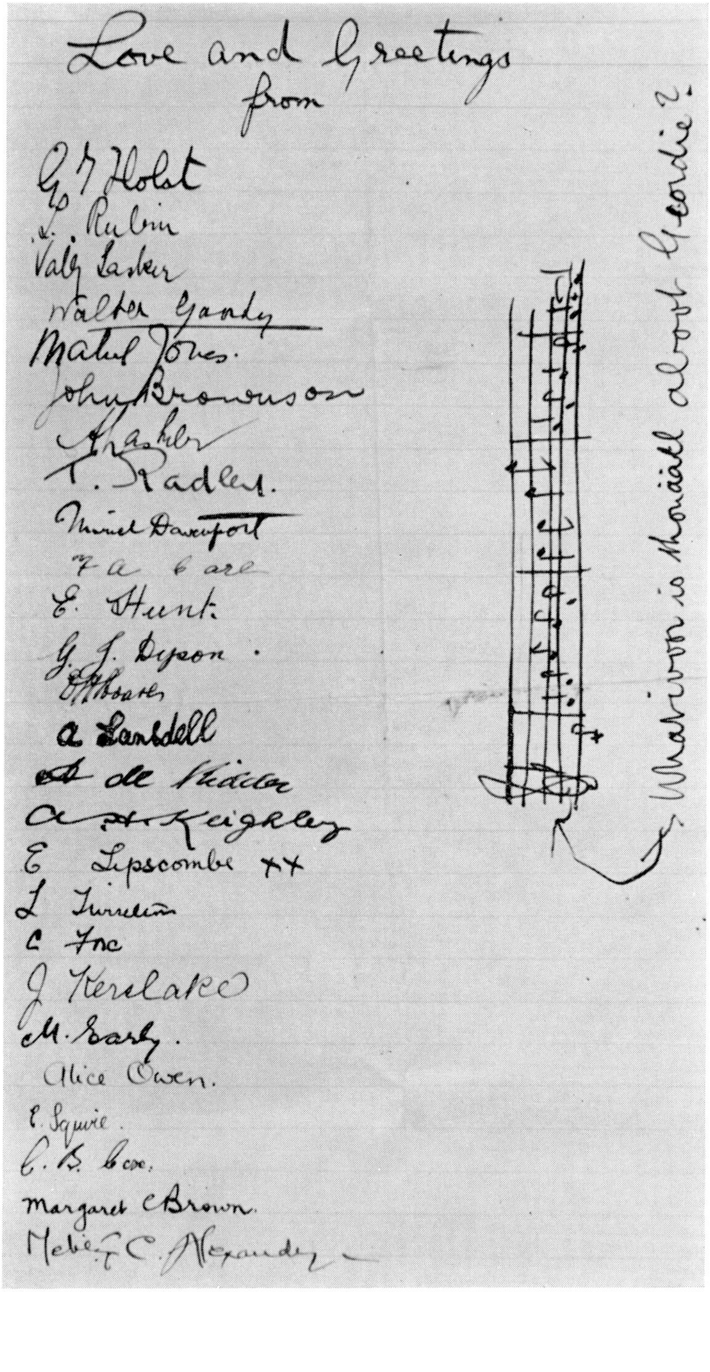
Love and Greetings
from
G. T. Holst
Vally Lasker
Walter Gandy
Mabel Jones.
John Bronwnson
Muriel Davenport
E. Hunt.
G. J. Dyson
A. Lansdell
E Lipscombe xx
J Kerslake
M. Early.
Alice Owen.
E. Squire.
C. B. Cox.
Margaret C Brown.
Whatever is this all about Geordie?

choral works; they have been a delightful experience, and one which I shall always remember with a thrill.

I am looking forward to the pleasure of seeing you again at the Birmingham performances in January.

With the best wishes of the coming season,

I am,

Yours truly,

W G Whittaker

---

¹ *Choral Hymns from the Rig Veda*: First Group, op. 26 [no. 1].

(b)

4 Granville Road,
Jesmond,
Newcastle on Tyne.

3/11/13

Dear von Holst,

It was a bold venture for our infant, which has only breathed eight weeks, to make its first appearance so. But the strong food has proved its very making. It has developed with quite surprising rapidity, a progress which would have been impossible had it been fed on milk-and-watery partsongy things, those namby-pamby trifles usually associated with ladies' choirs. I will not say that the performance was in any way worthy of the music, but the members worked with great enthusiasm, and sang the Hymns better than many an ancient choir would have done. Very many thanks for such splendidly original writings, so full of real beauty, so sincere and genuine. We shall most certainly take up the second set next season, and I shall hope that for the third of our existence, there will be another group of a set work from your pen for our enjoyment. We commenced "The Cloud Messenger" at College yesterday, so that the name of von Holst has loomed large in my little sphere this week.

This winter has proved so terribly busy that I have not yet got the Ode¹ arranged for piano and strings. However, things slacken in a fortnight, then I hope to get to work and return you the score in a short time. Your list of addresses will also come back to you in a few days.

Thanks muchly for your cheery note of this week.

Yours very truly,

W G Whittaker

---

¹ i.e. *The Cloud Messenger*, op. 30.

(c)
4 Granville Road,
Jesmond,
Newcastle on Tyne.

28/3/16

My Dear v H,

After another term's rehearsing of the Rig Veda set[1] (it is the second time now that I have prepared them for performance) I feel that every word I said to you about them two or three years ago requires only to be underlined. The choir made faces over them at the beginning, but came to love them, and sang them tonight with tremendous enthusiasm. We had about 110 women in the choir, and a very sympathetic pianist, and we all thoroughly enjoyed them. The audience were much delighted, particularly those who had taken part in "The Cloud Messenger".

I took one liberty, of making the semichorus sing the closing three Solo phrases in the "Travellers",[2] because I found that when a solitary voice came in, it sounded almost like a mistake. Pardon me for being heretical on the matter and for liking my distortion better.

We are coming up on the 7th for the Oriana and leaving on the 11th, at night. Will you send your soprano solo Rig Vedas[3] and any other songs of your own that you think most of to Miss Dorothy Silk, 21 Salisbury Rd, Moseley, Birmingham? She is a beautiful artist and woman, and is keen on singing the best things. She was asking about your songs tonight, and I promised to write you.

Again, gratitude from us all for your splendid things.

Yours ever,

W G Whittaker

[1] *Choral Hymns from the Rig Veda*: Third Group, op. 26 [no. 3].
[2] *Hymn of the Travellers*: no. 4 of the Third Group of *Choral Hymns from the Rig Veda*.
[3] *Vedic Hymns*, op. 24.

(d)
4 Granville Road,
Jesmond,
Newcastle on Tyne.

19/5/17

My Dear v H,

Do not think me a pessimist, or a "worrit" (North-country for a person who worries) if I detail some woes. The bass line has given me no end of anxiety, only two of those men were at the third concert, and some of the new ones were so hastily gathered into the fold that they were much below par. Duties, military and otherwise, have played the deuce with their attendance. Then the women-folk began to get the blues, and at the final rehearsal last night, they trembled like the light in a Crooks tube, and prophesied disaster wholesale for today.

The concert was at 3/0. At 1/0 came a note from Wall,[1] asking if we could do without him, he had got the "flues", a favourite thing with him, badly. He didn't know whether he could turn out. We should have had to cut out the trios. I didn't, for the life of me, know what could be put in instead, and the CM would have had to be done without strings at all, as missing out one would have meant doing without all. So I wrote back an imperative command for him to come. I trembled until he appeared at the hall, not knowing what to do without him. He had a temperature and no mistake, but he avowed his determination to get through at whatever cost. (Drop him a card and tell him he was a brick. "Cremona", Clayton Rd, Newcastle. He really was.)

Then the tambourine was a little sixteen-year old pupil of mine, a keen original piece of goods. The tympani was a mere boy from the barracks, supplied by Windram,[2] with no experience of anything outside of a military band. But the sole remaining percussion was playing from a marked piano copy, so her other job was to call out to him all the numbers, and she kept him absolutely straight at the rehearsal. Just before the CM she went to get her tambourine, which she had left in the cloakroom. Now we had the cloakroom locked, naturally, and the caretaker, THE caretaker, your particular friend, had the key. We instituted enquiries, but found that the beggar had GONE HOME. We sent somebody in search of him, and began, as she had nothing to do for a few minutes. We calculated that the tympani would manage for the first few pages. About halfway through she slid in to her seat, with a face as scarlet as could be, looking exhausted, and I found that the boy required a fair amount of pulling in and keeping out. However, the tambourine came in. It turned out that the caretaker couldn't be found, so the little woman had run to a music shop in the centre of the town, hatless, and in her party frock, borrowed a tambourine, run back, and got in exhausted. She played her part from memory, and well too. The copy was keeping company with the much locked, bolted, and barred instrument. You can imagine the excitement.

But to get to serious matters, the thing went better than I had hoped. AND, the audience seemed to like it greatly. The people I have seen, Windram, my mother, and others, said that they found the CM extremely beautiful, and were impressed immensely by it. One old weird critic, who writes for the "Yorkshire Post" when Herbert Thomson cannot come through, told one of the choir that the performance was a great improvement on the College one. The said choir member modestly and forcibly suggested that the difference might have been in the listener, as he knew something more about it.

I shall know better next week what the audience at large thought of it. The choir was tremendously keen on it, more than I can tell you. We had the largest audience we have yet had, Hadow[3] was there (I was surprised and delighted) and quite a decent beat up of the people who matter. The "Message" is one of the loveliest bits of writing you have done. It goes right to my heart.

You may be interested to know that our two young hopefuls voted the CM the nicest thing of the afternoon, but that Madrigals are dull. They are quite sure they never will like Madrigals.

How wonderful those Elizabethan things are. The Gibbons is most extraordinary; the Weelkes had to be repeated, the first encore in the history of the concerts.

Next week, I shall send you a few collected opinions, so that you may see that I'm not a voice crying in the wilderness.

I shall soon be "bereft of her who is my second self". My wife has had a complete nervous and physical breakdown (last week end we had a most anxious time) and the doctor says she must go to Bournemouth for at least a month. She comes south on Wed. The kiddies go to the school boarding house. We have no maid, I shall have to grub along as well as I can.

Today has been a melancholy day for my wife, she had wanted so much to hear the CM.

Now about Miss Lawton's piano, that will have to be continued in our next.

(*unsigned*)

[1] Alfred M. Wall.
[2] James Causley Windram.
[3] William H. Hadow.

(e)   4 Granville Rd,
                                                            Jesmond,
                                                            Newcastle on Tyne.

                                                            20/3/19

My Dear Holst,

Everything seems to show that The Planets have made the biggest impression of any of your things up till now. More than one personal account has come to me, and all are impressed by their bigness, their originality, and their beauty. For instance, Dunhill,[1] whom I saw recently, was carried away with them, and spoke in glowing terms.

Heartiest of Congratulations. You have had a rare long time to wait, but at last you are coming into your own. How I wish I could have heard them! Dionysus² is now a thing of the past. We had a terrible time with it, the women told me often that if they hadn't known and loved other things of yours they would never have had the courage to carry it through. But they WERE bricks. We used to work at it till they could sing no more, then do folksongs for a rest, then come back to Bacchus.³ And so on. I got to like it much better towards the end. Some parts I cannot yet reconcile myself to, but a great deal that was ungrateful before became more get-at-able. I won't say the performance was perfect. There were two very narrow squeaks, only saved from being catastrophes by two inexplicable miracles. It went with tremendous zest and fury, and the audience liked it hugely. They made a huge noise after it, and all reports today say that it really proved popular. One person told me beforehand that she would loathe it at first hearing, she always did loathe your things at first, but loved them on acquaintance. But she enjoyed it unaffectedly. The dear old lady who plays the contrabass for me everywhere told me afterwards that she only understood and enjoyed two modern composers, you and Frank Bridge. So you see my daring was rewarded.

Possibly your good lady has told you of the trouble about the band parts. I finally had to dish up an arrangement with the existing string parts. It wasn't satisfactory, but S and B only replied definitely that the quintet plus piano version was not available a few days before the concert. So I had to make the best of circumstances. I feel as if you had now paid me out for keeping those Cloud Messenger percussion parts so long.

Last night marked the end of the women's voice choir, the last concert out of College, and the close of my twentyfirst season of conductorship, so my dear girls were no end excited. We had presentations and speechifying the evening before, and everyone felt hilarious. They were greatly tickled at the thought of singing that wild Bacchic frenzy in a Temperance Hall. The note was written by the Professor of Classics, who is acting as Principal in Hadow's absence, so we were blest officially.

We are still without a Town Hall, and are likely to be. However, the Choral Union are going to give their affair in the Cathedral. It will take the form of a Peace concert. We shall do, possibly with strings, tymp, and organ, Parry's "Voces Clamantium", and Elgar's "Te Deum" and "Benedictus", and possibly some string or string and organ numbers, Davies' Solemn Melody, Elgar's Elegy and Sursum Corda, Bridge's Lament, and, I hope, Vaughan Williams' Fantasia on Themes by Tallis. I am right glad to be having a show of my own, the first one in all these long years. If we cannot get the Town Hall again next season, I have suggested that we give some motet performances in the Cathedral. In that case, H C will still not be coming through, there won't be funds to pay him. Most of the committee are most anxious that I shall have a show this season, it is encouraging to find so much sympathy and good will.

We had a gorgeous concert last week by the Catterall String Quartet. They are amongst the very best, they played the Beethoven Op 131, in C Sharp Minor superbly. It all seemed clear as noonday, and one wondered why it had ever been deemed obscure! We've made these chamber concerts pay, at cheap rates, 1/3 and 3/0, including tax. We had 600 people there, and the cheaper seat people, most of whom were new to chamber music, were enthusiastic. So it looks as if the Bach choir would have to run 9 concerts next season, 4 chamber and 5 choral. All this is very cheering, but it doesn't mean that I get more time to myself. Everything, in fact, works the other way. However, I mustn't growl.

I hear you are in Constantinople, but as no official change of address has been sent, this blather will be sent to the old one.

Regards, and happy times be yours.

Ever yours,

W G Whittaker

P.S. An old pupil of yours, a Miss Gotch (I think) was at the concert last night.

[1] Thomas F. Dunhill.
[2] *Hymn to Dionysus*, op. 31 no. 2.
[3] The words of the *Hymn to Dionysus* are taken from Gilbert Murray's translation of the *Bacchae* of Euripides.

(f)
4 Granville Road,
Jesmond,
Newcastle upon Tyne.

2nd December, 1926

My Dear Gustav,

I wish the performance had been more note-perfect, but there were really only two or three places where intonation beat the choir, but as far as the spirit was concerned it was really splendid. It sounded perfectly glorious; the climaxes were most thrilling.

Of course, we do not take any notice of the man who writes these reports, but the whole thing is very amusing. When you came here for the "Hymn of Jesus", he solemnly cursed you with bell, book and candle, and finished up with the remark—"For people who like this sort of thing, this is the sort of thing they will like"! Now he falls on his knees! We had a miserably small audience, but an enthusiastic one.

I am looking forward to seeing you on Wednesday morning at breakfast.

Ever yours,

Will

(g)

The Scottish National
Academy of Music,
St George's Place,
Glasgow, C.2.

17th February 1932.

My Dear Gustav,

You will see that we were thinking of you last night.

I intended having a boiled-down score, but three weeks ago Curwen informed me that the score and all parts were in America, so you not only go to U.S.A., but you take everything else with you! There was nothing for it but concocting a version for a small organ, piano and timps.

When the choir began the Fantasia[1] they hated it, but they gradually turned round and became most enthusiastic. Last night they really did sing the thing from the inside. It was one of the best choral performances of your works I have ever conducted. We had about eighty, fairly good balance, and lovely fresh voices.

The work appeals to me very strongly. It seems to me to be the best thing you have done of recent years.

I hope you are having a happy time.

Ever Yours,

Will

P.S. The enclosed report is [by] Percy Gordon, who knows what he is talking about.

[1] *A Choral Fantasia*, op. 51.

APPENDIX 5

The main addresses from which Holst wrote the letters in this book are given here in full.

(a) 10 The Terrace, Barnes, London SW (now SW13). This house has a commemorative plaque recording Holst's residence there between 1908 and 1913.
(b) 10 Luxemburg Gardens, Hammersmith, London W (now W6).
(c) St Paul's Girls' School, Brook Green, Hammersmith, London W (subsequently W6). From 1914 onwards, after the opening of the new

music room at the school, Holst often used St Paul's Girls' School headed notepaper for his letters, although they were not always written there. Sometimes he would use the notepaper while staying at other addresses, particularly at Thaxted, so that the replies would be sent to the school, where he taught on certain days of the week.

(d) Morley College (For Working Men & Women), Waterloo Road, London SE (subsequently SE1). At the time Holst wrote, Morley College classes were held in rooms at the rear of the Royal Victoria Hall (the 'Old Vic') in the Waterloo Road. It was not until 1924 that the College moved into its own building on the present site in Westminster Bridge Road.

(e) Thaxted, Essex. From 1914 to 1917, Holst lived at The Cottage, Monk Street, Thaxted, and from 1917 to 1925 at the Steps, Thaxted, although letters to his friends often omitted the full address and were headed simply 'Thaxted'.

(f) 32 Gunterstone Road, Barons Court, London W14.

(g) Brook End, Easton Park, Dunmow, Essex.

(h) Hill Cottage, Great Easton, Dunmow, Essex.

INDEX OF NAMES AND WORKS